IMAGES
of America

FIRST UNITED
METHODIST CHURCH
OF SAN DIEGO

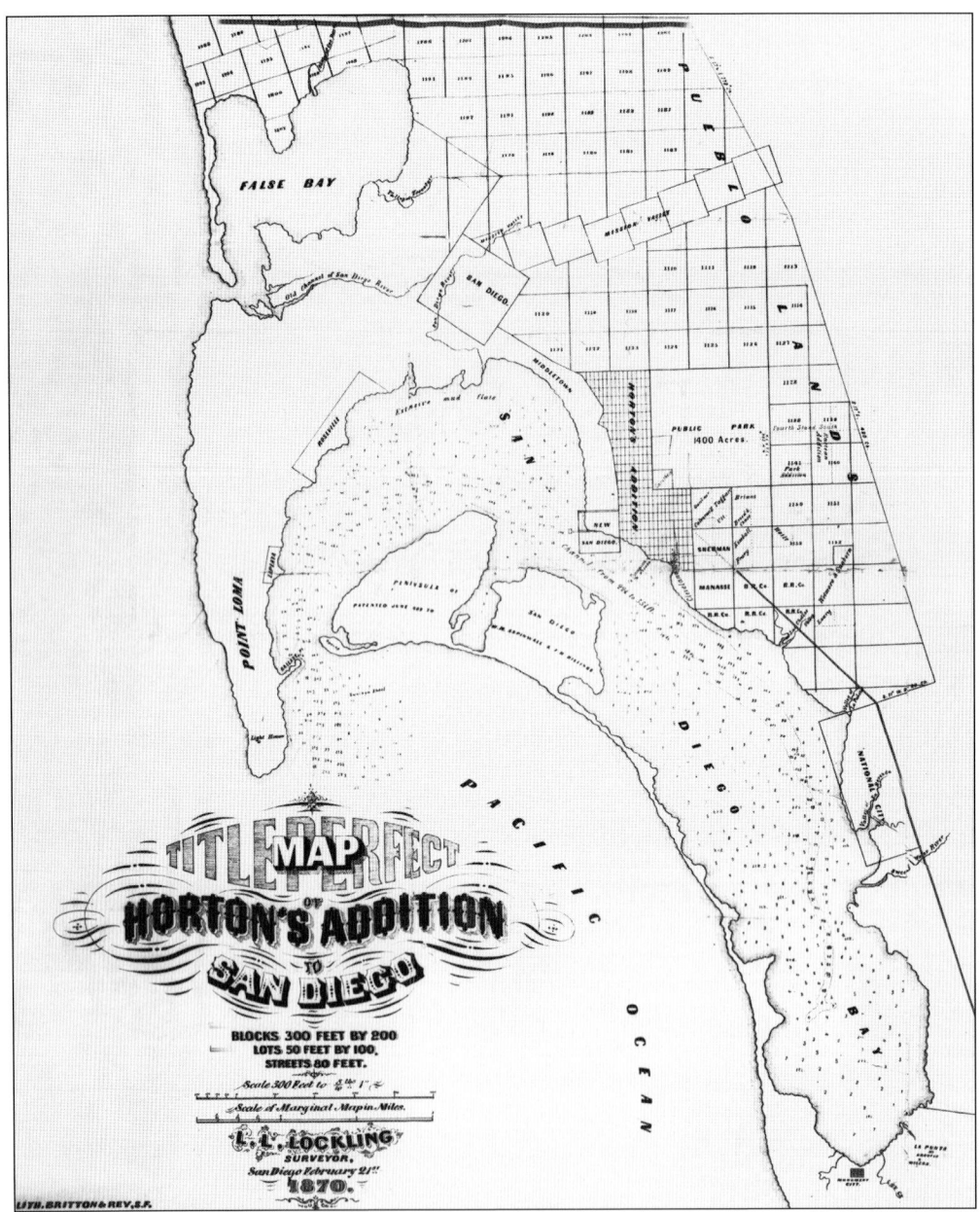

After Alonzo E. Horton arrived in San Diego, he purchased land just over the hills to the south of Old Town near the San Diego Harbor in April 1867 and established "Horton's Addition," or "New Town," shown on this map from 1870. New Town was where San Diego's Methodist Society decided to build its first church. (San Diego History Center.)

ON THE COVER: The military has been an integral part of the First United Methodist Church of San Diego ("First Church") congregation for over 100 years. As far back as World War I, First Church helped to entertain members of the armed forces. This c. 1918 photograph shows dozens of soldiers, sailors, and marines assembled with members of the congregation in front of the sanctuary at Ninth and C Streets, where the church was located from 1907 until 1964. (San Diego History Center.)

IMAGES
of America

FIRST UNITED
METHODIST CHURCH
OF SAN DIEGO

Krista Ames-Cook

ARCADIA
PUBLISHING

Published by Arcadia Publishing
Charleston, South Carolina

Printed in the United States of America

Library of Congress Control Number: 2018952265

For all general information, please contact Arcadia Publishing:
Telephone 843-853-2070
Fax 843-853-0044
E-mail sales@arcadiapublishing.com
For customer service and orders:
Toll-Free 1-888-313-2665

Visit us on the Internet at www.arcadiapublishing.com

*To the cloud of witnesses—the believers and pioneers—
who have served in San Diego and beyond since
that first Methodist prayer meeting in 1869.
To those who continue to inspire us to grow
in grace and to reach out in love.*

CONTENTS

ACKNOWLEDGMENTS

This book was originally inspired by Violet Emslie Knudtson's *Landmark of a Century*, affectionately called "The Red Book" because of its red cloth cover, which was published in 1969 for the centennial celebration of the First United Methodist Church of San Diego (First Church, or First UMC). For the sesquicentennial (150th) anniversary in 2019, I wanted to capture the church's history through vintage photographs and informative captions. I knew that Arcadia Publishing would be the ideal partner for this endeavor, and I appreciate the entire First UMC of San Diego staff, both past and present, who were champions for this project and helped make this book a reality.

Several church members provided great help by donating photographs and sharing their stories. Specifically, I would like to thank John Hermann, Bruce and Cheryl Johnson, LuAnn and Nancy Wherry, and Tom Myers for their contributions. A special thank-you to Sarah Bishop-Dolbec, who was an integral part of the historical committee in 2014 and helped with many tasks such as organizing and cataloging photographs and memorabilia in the church archives. I would also like to thank Cynthia Robertson for her guidance and input on the timeline and grouping of chapters.

Thank you to the San Diego History Center staff and the volunteers of the Ocean Beach Historical Society. Their research libraries, archives, and photograph collections offer a treasure trove of fascinating stories and information about San Diego's history.

Several church members paved the way for this book. Lucille Hildreth Wherry, Ethel D. Imel, Richard H. Peerson, and Harriett Loros all served on the First Church Historical Society/Committee in the past few decades and left a legacy through their research, writing, and enthusiasm for this church's history.

Last but not least, thank you to my family and friends for their encouragement and love. You are my foundation and I appreciate your steadfast support and belief in me.

Unless otherwise noted, all images appear courtesy of the First United Methodist Church of San Diego Archives. Thank you to the church members, local entities, and community groups who have donated photographs, historical memorabilia, and personal stories to the archives through the years. Photographs that appear courtesy of San Diego History Center are indicated with "SDHC" where appropriate.

INTRODUCTION

Wow, 150 years! That seems like a long time, but then we realize that there are still a few of us around who have been part of the life of this church for more than half of that time. In fact, a handful have been around for four generations: the Johnson, Myers, and Wherry families.

As of the time this book was written (June 2018), there are 26 individuals whose membership dates to before the church's move from Ninth and C Streets to the present Mission Valley site in 1964. They are George Barker, Bruce Barr, Mary Bryant, Ann Collica, Elizabeth DeTellem, Linda Dotson, Judy Fortin, Ellie Ghio, Barbara Gilbert, Lois Gruber, John Hermann, Liz Holcomb, Carol (Hoy) Holmgren, Bruce Johnson, Ida Manning, Connie Milam, Cynthia Miller, Tom Myers, Flavella Orton, Nardia Packer, Janice Peerson, Kirk Sheldon, Alice (Frazier) Staninger, Ross Stone, Nancy Wherry, and Sally Witucki.

We all know that the real life of the church has nothing to do with the various locations and buildings that it has occupied during this period of 150 years. Our church is very fortunate to have been served by many outstanding and inspiring preachers through all these years—not one dud in the whole string of them! But the life and health of a church is best told by the activity the church is involved in and the groups, classes, guilds, and societies that provide fellowship, education, leadership opportunities, and global and community service. Each generation has seen the ups and downs of such organizations based on which ones best fit within the particular time and cultural setting.

The history of the first few decades of the church chronicles Bible studies, inviting other community groups and organizations to share the church's facilities, and church members becoming actively involved in civic affairs. During the middle third of our history, adult Sunday school classes played a prominent role. Some of those key groups were the Wesleyan class, the Challengers class, and the Voyagers class. These had large and loyal memberships and were incubators for most of the key leadership positions in the church. Those groups are now gone, but there is currently a very strong group called Koinonia.

Small, informal groups have always played a key role. For example, years ago, Mother's Morning Out provided a few hours of respite for young mothers. They later became Mothers Together. This circle filled the need for young mothers to share childcare ups and downs, Bible study, community service, and probably a little bragging. The group evolved after those needs expired but continues on 40 years later as a close-knit circle of church friends who still meet regularly and now share the enjoyment of grandchildren. There are many similar examples of such groups.

Women in the church have always been the "works" that kept the church ticking. This not only provided leadership and fellowship, but was often an accidental way to get the men and children of the church involved too. In the early decades, this took the form of the Ladies Aid Society and missionary guilds. For example, the Helen Ferris Guild was created to support Helen Ferris, the daughter of Dr. Lincoln Ferris, minister from 1917 to 1924, when Helen was a missionary in China. The Helen Ferris Guild was still going strong into the 1960s. The Women's Society for Christian Service was a driving force. Church members held rummage sales, bazaars (craft fairs), potluck dinners, and fashion shows, and hosted receptions. These activities raised a lot of money for missions and other projects. All-church socials (the best potlucks ever) were regularly held in the basement of the church at Ninth and C Streets and featured multigenerational games, fun and laughter, and finishing the celebration with a huge friendship circle while holding hands and singing "Blest Be the Tie That Binds"—a great tradition long gone.

In the early years, Methodist youth belonged to the Young Peoples Methodist Alliance, which later became the Epworth League. It was then called Methodist Youth Fellowship (MYF). District-wide youth activities were popular, from Youth Day at Annual Conference (Bishop Gerald Kennedy was a very popular and charismatic youth leader at that time) to district-wide dances and Easter and summer camps at Camp Cedar Glen and Camp Virginia. There were athletic leagues filled with church teams from within the district. The church at Ninth and C Streets was the recipient of many sets of roller skates from a defunct roller rink, and the entire church basement was set up as a roller rink! This led to many fun times, as might be imagined. The church conference provided opportunities for college-aged summer work teams to travel to mission fields. Several friends participated in such a team to the Congo, and another team traveled to Italy. Wesley Fellowship (college-age) was a strong program from 1955 to 1962, as it was home to countless servicemen and college students (many love matches came out of this group). These youth programs often led to life-changing experiences.

While in college, Bruce Johnson was hired one summer as church custodian. One of his most unique jobs was climbing up through the belfry onto the top of the rotating cross (see page 46) to change the light bulbs. There was a great view of the bay and everything for miles around that only he and the seagulls were privileged to enjoy.

It is no secret that our times are changing. They always have. Just study the history in this book, and you will see problems, triumphs, and crises through the years. It is almost as if history repeats itself. And yet, this church has always come through stronger and more dedicated to our mission in our community and in the world. It kind of makes you wonder what the next 50 years will hold. What will be the names of the new adult classes? What small groups will start that will lead to long-lasting friendships? Will the church operate out of even more locations? How will our community service evolve? What new pastors will inspire and challenge us? Where do we want to be in 50 years?

—Bruce and Cheryl Johnson

One

HUMBLE BEGINNINGS
SEARCHING FOR A CHURCH HOME
(1869–1887)

In 1869, San Diego was a sleepy little town awakening from 100 years of serving as a trading town for merchant ships. One hundred years earlier, in 1769, the first Spanish mission was founded, and the pueblo ("village" or "little town") of San Diego was established in the area now known as Old Town. The early settlers came to the area after receiving land grants from the Spanish and Mexican governments to build ranchos. The discovery of gold near Sacramento in 1848 and the gold rush that followed in 1849 brought people west to California as they began seeking new opportunities.

After California became a state on September 9, 1850, more people started coming to the little town of San Diego, which held such promise. In 1850, the US Army established a base in San Diego and built some barracks along the waterfront. During the 1860s, many came to visit, and some chose to stay and make San Diego their home. It was during this period, in 1867, when Alonzo Horton, a San Francisco furniture dealer, came to San Diego and established Horton's Addition, or New Town, just over the hills to the south of Old Town. Horton's vision for New Town included businesses that would have greater convenience for ships arriving in San Diego Bay from the East. He also organized the streets to have short blocks so he would have more corner land lots.

As Horton was building his New Town, many people noted that San Diego had no Protestant church facilities. On February 6, 1869, a handful of people gathered in an upper room at an unoccupied Army barracks for a Methodist prayer meeting. This was the beginning of the Methodist Society in San Diego.

Following the first prayer meetings in the barracks, the growing Methodist Society looked for a permanent home after meeting at venues along Fifth Street, first above a saloon and then above some members' stores. In that first year, the Methodist Society officially became consecrated as a new congregation of the First Methodist Episcopal (M.E.) Church on May 12, 1869, and continued its services at Dunham Hall on the second floor above the post office. According to many accounts, the First M.E. Church was the first Protestant church in San Diego County.

In 1850, an Army supply depot for Southern California was established along the bay in San Diego, and quarters were built for the soldiers. The barracks, located at H (now Market) and Arctic (now Kettner) Streets, were unoccupied when it was used as the site for the Methodist Society's first prayer meeting in February 1869. This c. 1889 photograph shows the waterfront with the Army barracks in the left foreground. (SDHC.)

Mrs. Case, a devout lady in her 70s, arranged for the Methodist prayer meeting in the barracks. On February 6, 1869, the humble group stood in the empty, candlelit room and listened to scriptures and a message from the local minister. A woman who attended wrote to her family, stating that only her faith helped her endure "this desolate corner of creation." This c. 1889 photograph shows the US Army using the barracks. (SDHC.)

After holding the first prayer meetings in the Army barracks and later ones at various venues along Fifth Street, the growing Methodist Society began to look for a permanent home. In the late 1860s, Fifth Street and the surrounding areas had dirt streets, sidewalks made from wood planks, and hitches to tie up horses. This c. 1870 photograph illustrates what Fifth Street looked like around that time. (SDHC.)

In March 1869, the Methodist Society moved its Sunday services to the second story of a building at the southwest corner of Fifth and H (now Market) Streets. However, a saloon did a thriving business on the first floor, which caused distractions. After a month, the fledgling church relocated again. The move in April 1869 was to the upper story of a plumbing store owned by church members A.H. Julian and Sons. This c. 1869 photograph shows A.H. Julian and some of his employees in front of the store at 528 Fifth Street. (SDHC.)

Dunham Hall was located at 748–758 Fifth Street and was built in 1869 by Columbus Dunham, a Methodist, pictured here in the white shirt and black tie. The small boy standing near him is his son George Robert Dunham. The Methodists met above the post office in this building from mid-1869 (around May) until moving into their own church building a couple of blocks away in February 1870. (SDHC.)

At the corner of Fourth and Broadway (formerly D) Streets, the newly formed Methodist Episcopal congregation constructed a simple church that could seat 300 worshippers. The church was built for just under $4,000, including a parsonage, and was dedicated debt-free on February 17, 1870. This c. 1872 photograph shows the white wooden church just beyond the *San Diego Union* building. (SDHC.)

Rev. E.S. Chase served as the minister of First Methodist Church from 1885 to 1888. The first wooden church was a small structure 35 feet wide by 50 feet long. Even with an additional 20 feet added to the church, by 1887, the need for a much larger building was evident. Under the leadership of Reverend Chase, the congregation decided to build a much larger brick square.

First Methodist Episcopal Church made history with a marriage-by-telegraph in 1876. The wedding took place on April 24, 1876, with the bride's family and Rev. Jonathan Mann at the telegraph office in San Diego while the engaged couple, Clara Choate and William Storey, were at a telegraph office in Arizona. This c. 1878 photograph shows the San Diego Western Union Telegraph building. (SDHC.)

On the edge of San Diego Bay, the area known as New Town, developed by Alonzo Horton, was full of promise for the future. Horton House, a hospitality establishment from around 1870 until 1905, was located where the U.S. Grant Hotel is today. This c. 1885 photograph shows a gathering of San Diegans in the plaza with Horton House on the left and the small, wooden Methodist Episcopal church next to it. (SDHC.)

By 1887 membership had increased, so the small wooden church was moved, and a large three-story building, the First Methodist Episcopal (M.E.) Church Block, was built in its place. The wooden church was relocated to a lot on Third Street between B and C Streets and used until the new church was ready. It was later moved and then demolished. This c. 1887 photograph shows the M.E. Church Block under construction. (SDHC.)

Two

THE M.E. CHURCH BLOCK
THE BRICK SQUARE
(1887–1906)

The original members of First Methodist Church in San Diego were not daunted by the town's primitive surroundings in the 1860s. After becoming fully organized on May 12, 1869, the members immediately began the undertaking of building a church sanctuary.

On the corner of Fourth Street and D Street (now Broadway), the congregation built a small white wooden church, 35 feet wide by 50 feet long, which was dedicated on February 17, 1870. In 1876, twenty more feet were added to the church, making it 35 by 70 feet, to accommodate the growing congregation. Times were prosperous, and by 1885, a bigger church was deemed necessary. From 1885 to 1887, plans were made to construct a second new First M.E. Church on the same site as the original white wooden church. The new edifice was also known as "The M.E. Church Block," "The Brick Square," and "The Brick Block."

The building campaign was called An Adventure in Faith because so much money was borrowed for its construction. The Brick Square was designed to have six spaces for stores on the first floor, 18 offices on the second and third floors, and a sanctuary with a couple of extra rooms for Sunday school, but no kitchen was provided. It was estimated that the sanctuary, located on the upper two floors, could seat 1,500 people.

When it was completed in 1888, the three-story M.E. Church Block was considered by many to be the finest building in San Diego. To pay for it, the Methodists planned that the rent from the stores and offices would bring in the necessary income. Yet this did not turn out as expected, and the church's debt increased. There were concerns of foreclosure on the church property, which would have brought about a total loss.

In 1892, a new minister was selected to come from Kansas to San Diego. However, Rev. L.M. Hartley thought he was coming to a prosperous church. When he realized the church's financial difficulties, Reverend Hartley went to work to save it. Through some clever fundraising, the congregation paid off the debt on the church. In 1896, a new 10-year mortgage was secured at better terms and with considerably reduced interest. The financial load was eased. In 1905, it was decided to sell the property one year before the mortgage expired.

By 1887, the church membership had increased to 395. It was then that a large three-story building, the First M.E. Church Block, was built in its place. The cost was $50,000 including the pipe organ. The structure was a combination church edifice on the second and third floors and income-producing commercial space on the street level. This building had six storefronts and 18 office rooms created for rent. (SDHC.)

The new church block, shown here in 1888, was planned in such a way that it would serve society for many purposes while also being a source of income for the church. The Brick Block was completed during the boom period of the late 1880s. The structure was considered to be the finest in the city. (SDHC.)

Rev. M.F. Colburn was the pastor of First M.E. Church from 1888 to 1892. It was near the end of his ministry that the Great Financial Panic started in 1892.

The church sanctuary was an auditorium on the second floor, and its ceiling reached to the top of the third floor. The auditorium was 65 feet wide and 100 feet long. It had a balcony that reached around three sides of the auditorium. The church also had a Sunday school room and a smaller room for children. There were no real kitchen facilities. This photograph shows the M.E. Church Block around 1890.

This image shows the "Brick Block" Methodist Episcopal church on Easter Sunday, March 25, 1894. This is one of the few known photographs that shows the inside of the Brick Block church. The sanctuary was on the second and third floors, with a full balcony extending to the top of the third floor. It was estimated the balcony and auditorium could seat 1,500 people.

When the Methodist Block was dedicated on February 26, 1888, San Diego was a thriving city of 30,000 people. Shortly thereafter, a severe eight-year drought started, and by 1891, the city's population fell to 16,000. In 1892, the Great Financial Panic struck, and the survival of First Church was at stake. The church was in debt, and foreclosure proceedings began. This c. 1896 photograph shows an unidentified man with his cart and donkey in Horton Plaza with the M.E. Church Block in the background. (SDHC.)

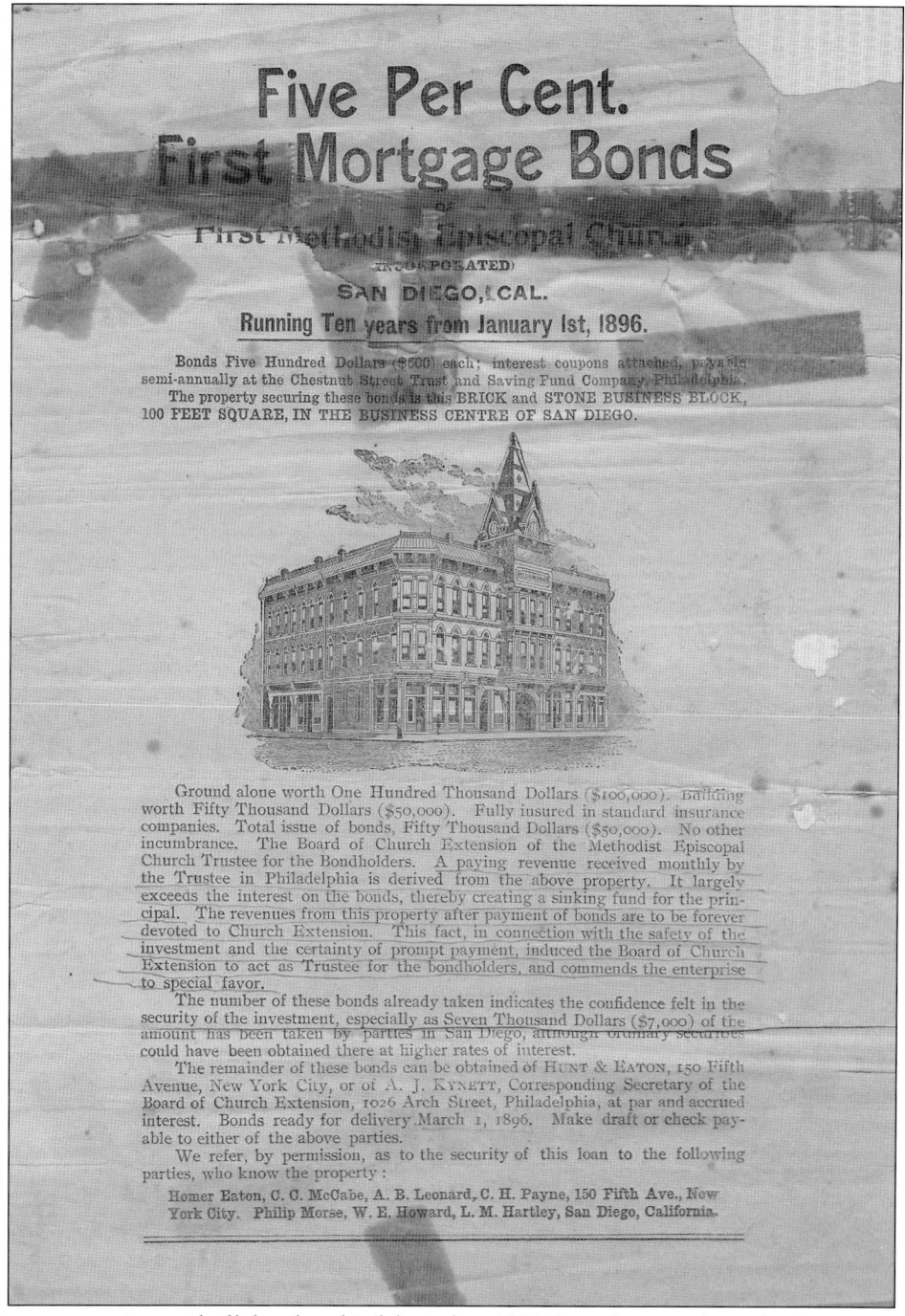

Five Per Cent.
First Mortgage Bonds
of
First Methodist Episcopal Church
(INCORPORATED)
SAN DIEGO, CAL.

Running Ten years from January 1st, 1896.

Bonds Five Hundred Dollars ($500) each; interest coupons attached, payable semi-annually at the Chestnut Street Trust and Saving Fund Company, Philadelphia. The property securing these bonds is this BRICK and STONE BUSINESS BLOCK, 100 FEET SQUARE, IN THE BUSINESS CENTRE OF SAN DIEGO.

Ground alone worth One Hundred Thousand Dollars ($100,000). Building worth Fifty Thousand Dollars ($50,000). Fully insured in standard insurance companies. Total issue of bonds, Fifty Thousand Dollars ($50,000). No other incumbrance. The Board of Church Extension of the Methodist Episcopal Church Trustee for the Bondholders. A paying revenue received monthly by the Trustee in Philadelphia is derived from the above property. It largely exceeds the interest on the bonds, thereby creating a sinking fund for the principal. The revenues from this property after payment of bonds are to be forever devoted to Church Extension. This fact, in connection with the safety of the investment and the certainty of prompt payment, induced the Board of Church Extension to act as Trustee for the bondholders, and commends the enterprise to special favor.

The number of these bonds already taken indicates the confidence felt in the security of the investment, especially as Seven Thousand Dollars ($7,000) of the amount has been taken by parties in San Diego, although ordinary securities could have been obtained there at higher rates of interest.

The remainder of these bonds can be obtained of HUNT & EATON, 150 Fifth Avenue, New York City, or of A. J. KYNETT, Corresponding Secretary of the Board of Church Extension, 1026 Arch Street, Philadelphia, at par and accrued interest. Bonds ready for delivery March 1, 1896. Make draft or check payable to either of the above parties.

We refer, by permission, as to the security of this loan to the following parties, who know the property :

Homer Eaton, C. C. McCabe, A. B. Leonard, C. H. Payne, 150 Fifth Ave., New York City. Philip Morse, W. E. Howard, L. M. Hartley, San Diego, California.

The congregation paid off the church's debt in late 1895 through some clever fundraising, such as serving 25¢-per-plate dinners, holding bazaars, and hosting lectures and entertainers. In 1896, a new 10-year mortgage was secured at better terms and lower interest rates, which considerably reduced the overall debt. At the time, the property was conservatively valued at $100,000. The mortgage of $50,000 was for 10 years at five percent interest. This is the mortgage bond, issued in January 1896, that helped the Methodist Brick Block church survive its financial crisis.

This unique photograph of a nearly deserted D Street, showing the Horton House and the M.E. Church Block behind it, was taken around 1899. To the right (out of the frame) is Horton Plaza. (SDHC.)

D Street, which ran in front of Horton House and the M.E. Church Block, was the civic center and was often used for city parades and events. This c. 1899 photograph shows a parade, possibly for the Grand Army of the Republic. The arch in the foreground somewhat hides First Church, but the clock tower is visible above it. (SDHC.)

The clock tower rose five stories and was a landmark of the downtown area. This photograph shows the M.E. Church Block in 1900. (SDHC.)

The church estimated that the rent from the stores and offices would produce the necessary income to pay for this building. However, this did not prove to be true. Throughout the period of the Methodist Block, the possible loss of the property kept ministers and the congregation in a state of constant anxiety. This c. 1905 photograph shows the M.E. Church Block looking northeast from D Street. (SDHC.)

By 1905, the trustees and congregation were motivated to make a change. The area around Fourth and D Streets was growing too noisy for worship services, and there was a desire to move away from the business area. (SDHC.)

On April 25, 1905, the Brick Block was sold to Ulysses Simpson "Buck" Grant Jr. for $100,000 net cost, subject to the $50,000 bonded indebtedness and subject to a deed from Alonzo Horton and Louis J. Wilde. After the sale, the church had free use of the space for six months, and the pipe organ was not included in the transaction. This 1905 photograph shows the Brick Block on the northeast corner of Fourth and D Streets and the remnants of the demolished Horton House in the foreground. (SDHC.)

In 1905, Horton House was demolished, and the U.S. Grant Hotel was built in its place. When Ulysses S. Grant Jr. bought the Methodist Block one year before the mortgage expired, there was enough profit left over to establish a building fund for a new church. Grant, the second son of Pres. Ulysses S. Grant, was an attorney and entrepreneur. This 1906 photograph shows the Methodist Block in the background and the foundation for the new hotel in the foreground. Next to the M.E. Church Block was the Pickwick Theater, designed by William Hebbard and Irving J. Gill and built in 1904. The Pickwick opened in February 1905 as a vaudeville theater and became a motion-picture theater in 1922. It had a short life as a movie theater and was demolished in 1926. (SDHC.)

Three

RELOCATION
A MOVE FROM PLAZA TO PASTURE
(1906–1918)

By 1905, the Brick Square, or M.E. Church Block, seemed to have weathered the financial stress of the previous 10 years. However, the congregation and trustees wanted to make a change because the area around Fourth Street and D Street (now Broadway) was growing too noisy for worship services, even though there was some nervousness about relocating farther away from the business area. Second, an opportunity to sell the church property for a profit seemed too good to pass up. The property was sold for $100,000, leaving a profit for the establishment of a building fund for a new, third church.

In April 1905, the Brick Square was sold to Ulysses S. Grant Jr. The church was to have free use of the auditorium, which was used as the sanctuary, and Sunday school rooms for a six-month period from the date of the last payment. It was understood that the pipe organ and other personal property of the church was not to be included in the sale. A committee was appointed to seek a site for a new church, one not so close to the center of the city yet not so far removed as to be inaccessible.

A new church site was selected at Ninth and C Streets. This choice was a disappointment to many members, since the location was considered to be out in the country. The plans for the new church building were designed by Irving J. Gill, an architect who did distinguished work in the late 19th and early 20th centuries. The plans that Gill presented to the First M.E. Church were Gothic Revival and represented his only effort in this style. The cornerstone for the new structure was laid on July 1, 1906, and it was completed and ready for dedication on May 5, 1907.

In 1908, a set of bells, or chimes, was gifted to the church by Dr. Gaylord H. Hartupee. His donation of the bells, although they would be in custody of the church, was heralded in the city as a gift to all the people of San Diego. When the bells were played by the carillonneur, the sound of the chimes floating over the city could be heard for many miles.

This 1906 photograph shows land preparation at Ninth and C Streets prior to the construction of the new church. The clock tower of the M.E. Church Block was visible in the distant skyline. When First Church moved in 1907, some said that they were moving "out to the pasture land," since this new site was so far removed from downtown. However, the sites were only one quarter-mile apart in distance.

The new church, designed by Irving J. Gill, was built on the outskirts of town. On July 1, 1906, the cornerstone of the building was laid. The tract cost the church $18,500, and the complete budget was $50,000. Certain portions of the basement and some other parts were left unfinished. The completed church was dedicated on May 5, 1907.

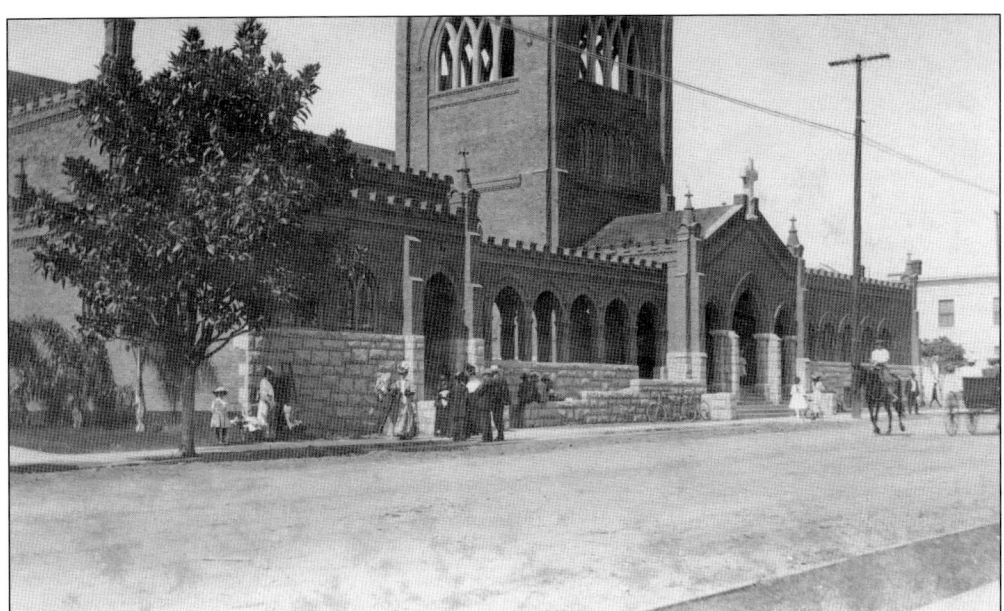

Found in a personal album, this c. 1907 photograph looks northeast on C Street and shows the Ninth and C Street church. James Simpson, who did the stone masonry work, also donated the cross above the main entrance on C Street. This photograph was possibly taken on a Sunday after church, as the people in front of the church seem to be dressed in their Sunday best. (SDHC.)

Irving John Gill, known as "Jack" to his friends, was considered a pioneer of the modern movement in architecture. He moved to San Diego in 1893 for health reasons and launched his own architecture studio specializing in the design of large residences in eclectic styles. Gill designed several buildings that are considered examples of San Diego's best architecture. Many of his designs throughout Southern California are designated as historic places. He is pictured here around 1915. (SDHC.)

Dedication Week, which occurred preceding May 5, 1907, was filled with activity at the new church, starting with a special fellowship rally and conference meeting on Wednesday evening. Friday night was filled with social events to which all members and friends were invited. This group of young men was photographed on the front steps of the new church. The cornerstone is visible behind the man at far right in the first row.

According to the reverse of this photograph from the church archives, it was taken in February 1907 by Ada Mossman and features a group of young ladies who stopped for a luncheon picnic on the road to San Diego Mission. Pictured are, from left to right, Sadie Farr, Blanche Jones, Zella Cherry, Leila Alexander, Blanche Bone, Martha Harris, and Crystobal McNamera.

Rev. Lewis T. Guild served as minister of the church from 1907 to 1911. A milestone in the history of the church was the publication of a bulletin prepared by Reverend Guild. The first copy was distributed on April 7, 1907, and proved to be popular. Members were encouraged to send extra copies to their friends in other cities.

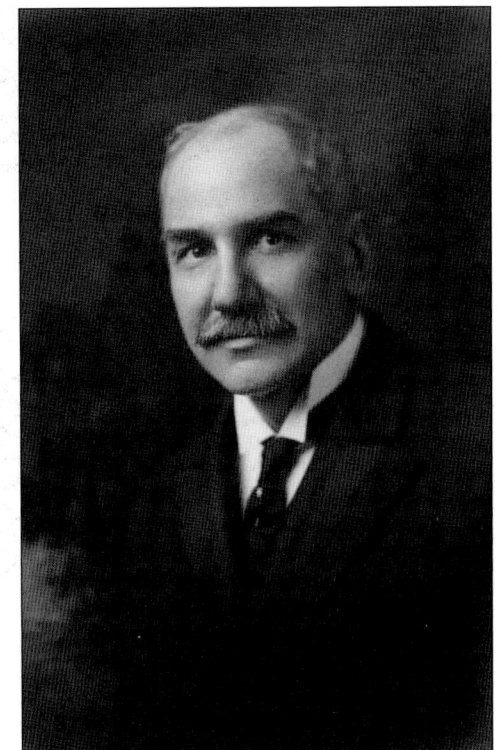

To help fund the new church at Ninth and C Streets, one fundraising effort included selling voluntary bonds for $36 each to be paid at the rate of $1 per month for three years. This is one of the bond certificates. Voluntary bond No. 202 was issued for $72 in January 1906. The seal at lower right reads "Paid in full—Jan. 10, 1909."

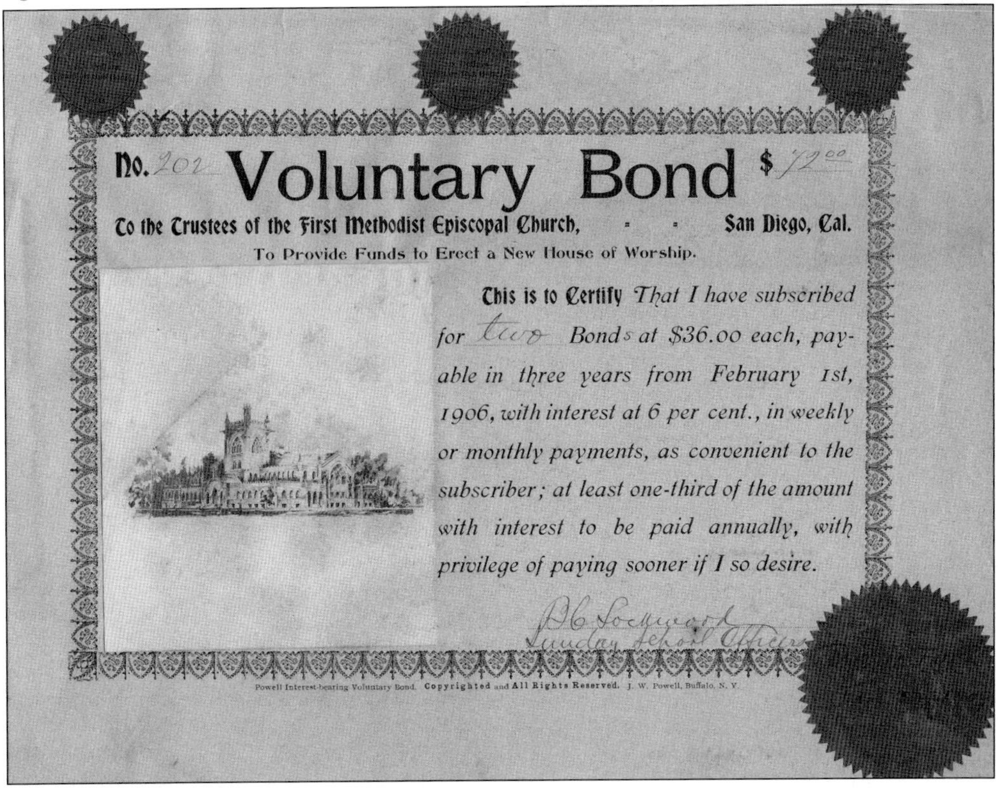

No. 202 **Voluntary Bond** $72.00

To the Trustees of the First Methodist Episcopal Church, San Diego, Cal.

To Provide Funds to Erect a New House of Worship.

This is to Certify *That I have subscribed for* two *Bonds at $36.00 each, payable in three years from February 1st, 1906, with interest at 6 per cent., in weekly or monthly payments, as convenient to the subscriber; at least one-third of the amount with interest to be paid annually, with privilege of paying sooner if I so desire.*

D. C. Lockwood
Sunday School Officers

Powell Interest-bearing Voluntary Bond. Copyrighted and All Rights Reserved. J. W. Powell, Buffalo, N. Y.

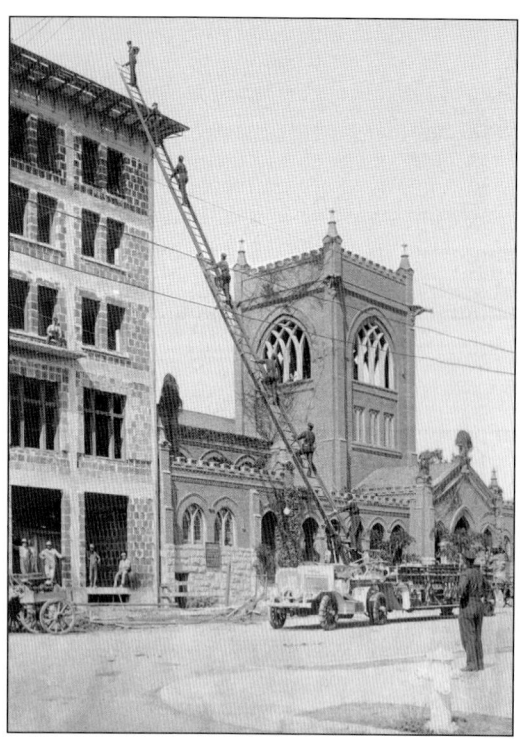

This c. 1910 photograph shows the Ninth and C Street church in the background with the San Diego Fire Department extinguishing a blaze in the five-story building next door. (SDHC.)

The First M.E. Church was built in the Gothic Revival style and represented Irving Gill's only effort in this style. The gothic theme was carried into the tower and distinguished by four gargoyles, which were the cause of some lively discussions during the building of the church. However, Gill declared that they were necessary to complete this type of architecture. Many members of the congregation insisted the gargoyles smacked of "heathen images." They were removed in the early 1940s during a remodeling of the exterior. This photograph shows the church in 1912. (SDHC.)

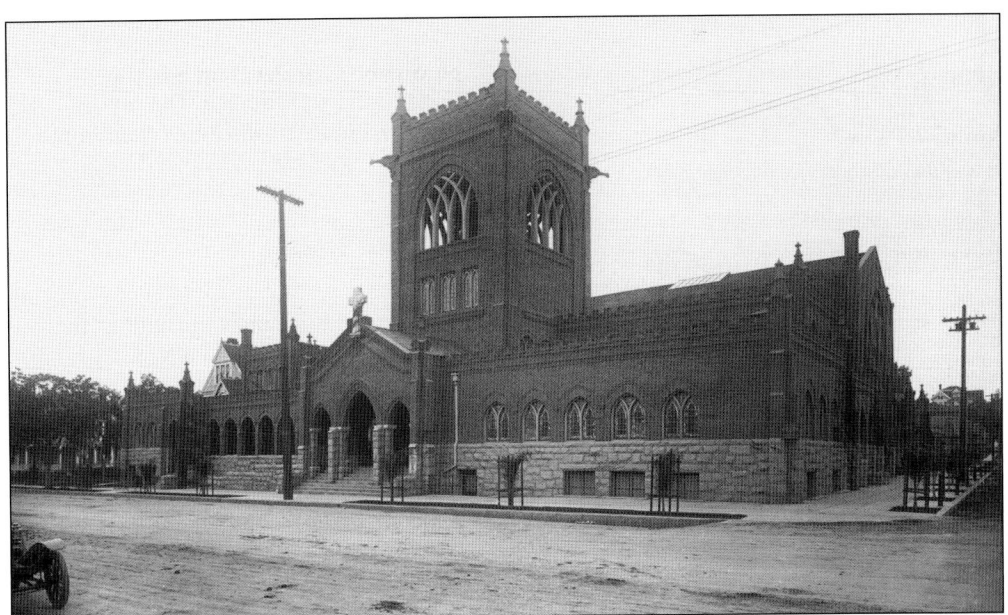

In 1908, Dr. Gaylord H. Hartupee gifted a set of bells, or chimes, to the M.E. Church of San Diego. The 11 bells, in the key of E, weigh 9,600 pounds, and the number of tunes that can be played is nearly limitless. When the carillonneur played the bells, the sound of the chimes floated over the city. This photograph shows the church and bell tower around 1913. (SDHC.)

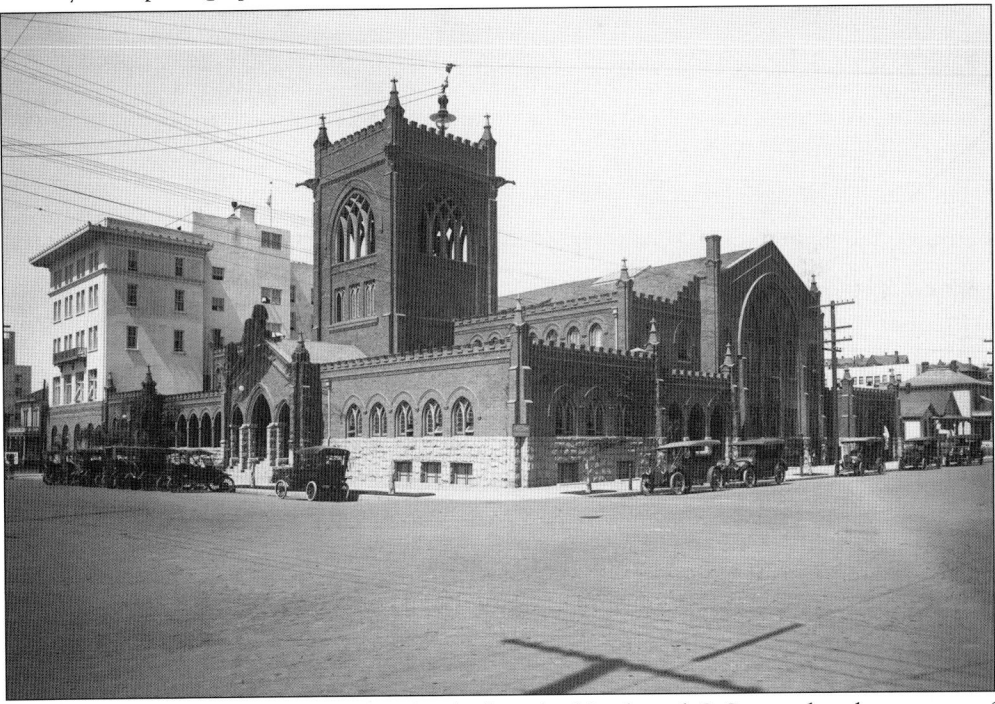

It was 1913 before the basement was finished in the Ninth and C Street church at a cost of $1,400. The basement functioned as both classrooms and a dining room. The layout of the church included the sanctuary and a balcony that encircled the altar. A large Sunday school auditorium and balcony could be opened to double the seating in the sanctuary. (SDHC.)

Rev. Richard D. Hollington served as minister from 1912 to 1916. He exchanged pastorates with Rev. Lewis T. Guild, who went to Toledo, Ohio. Reverend Hollington was said to be eloquent and popular, although there is no record of the kind of sermons he preached.

The site was a 100-by-150-foot property at the corner of Ninth and C Streets. The church, dedicated in May 1907, was built for $100,000—double the original budget. The beautiful and functional building featured gothic architecture, stained-glass windows, a magnificent pipe organ, a graceful bell tower, and a soft wood interior. This c. 1914 photograph shows the church during its 45th year of ministry in San Diego. (SDHC.)

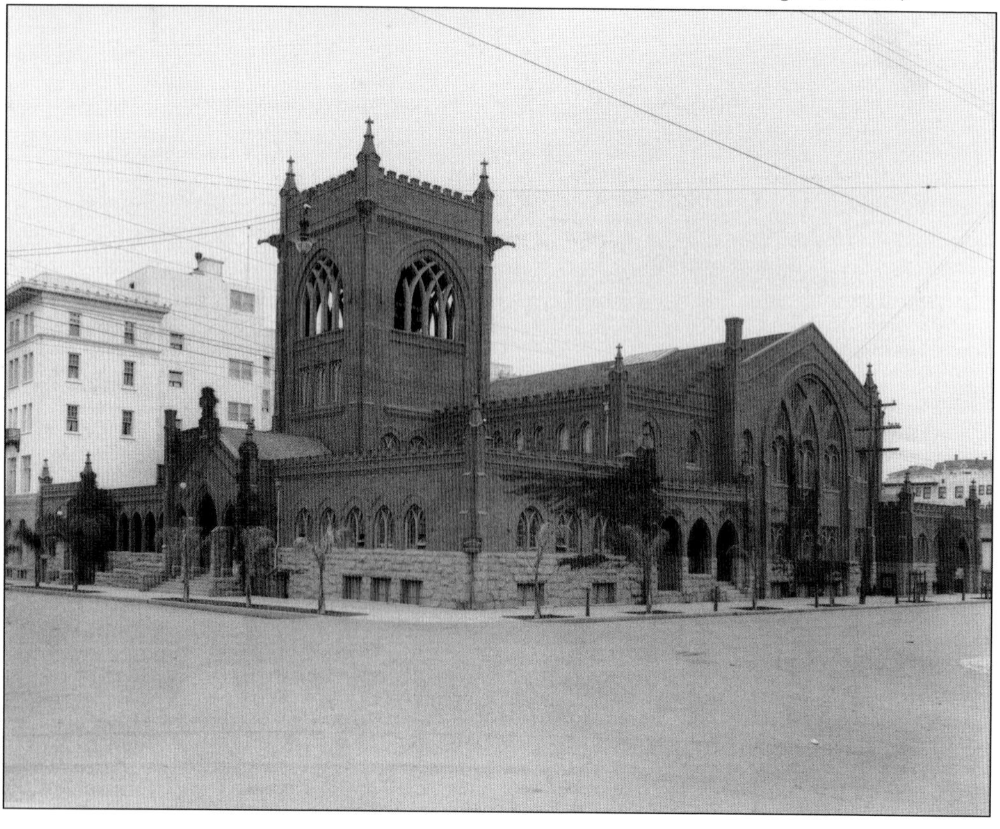

The Ninth and C Street church is pictured on Easter Sunday, April 12, 1914. The organ that had been in the Brick Square was a two-manual Hook and Hastings instrument dedicated on February 26, 1888. When the previous church building was sold, the organ was retained and moved to the new church at Ninth and C Streets. The Hook and Hastings instrument was enlarged and installed in the 1,500-seat auditorium. This organ was used until 1929. (SDHC.)

The Friendship Class, for single young men, is pictured in 1914 at the Ninth and C Street church. According to a note on the reverse, this photograph was presented to the church by Herbert E. Brunkow (standing at far right in the back row).

One of the many ministries of First M.E. Church was this Social Service Department. This c. 1916 photograph shows a large home that served as the headquarters. The sign above the porch indicated that the site offered a free reading room. The exact location of this building is unknown; however, it was most likely near the Ninth and C Street church.

In 1916, the First M.E. Church of San Diego provided social services for those in need by offering beds, meals, and medical care. In addition to dorm-style sleeping quarters for men and women, private bedrooms, a clinic, a reading room, a dining room, and a reception room, the Social Service Department also had a Clothing Room, shown here in 1916. It offered clothes for men, women, and children.

In November 1916, the Social Service Department workers and residents gathered to share a meal for Thanksgiving. More than 20 people enjoyed this holiday meal.

This 1912 photograph shows the completed U.S. Grant Hotel with the Brick Block across the street and a flourishing Horton Plaza. At this point, the Methodists were worshipping in their new location uptown at Ninth and C Streets. The former church site was used by various businesses from 1907 until it was demolished in 1913. (SDHC.)

The designer of the fountain in Horton Plaza was Irving Gill, the same architect who designed the Ninth and C Street church. Alonzo Horton gave the plaza to San Diego in 1870. In 1908, Gill's fountain design was the winner of a competition that included 12 other entries. A key requirement was that the fountain be equipped with an electrical apparatus that would project blended colors on spraying water. The fountain is pictured here in 1911. (SDHC.)

This 1913 photograph was taken after the Methodist church had moved. It shows the M.E. Church Block shortly before it was demolished and replaced with the Owl Drug Company building in 1914. Compared to the 1905 photograph on page 22, the change in modes of transportation in less than 10 years is notable.

PHOTOGRAPH OF FOUNTAIN
IN PLAZA SAN DIEGO CAL
COLDEST DAY ON RECORD
TEM. 22° JAN. 7. 1913

The note written on this image states: "Photograph of Fountain in Plaza, San Diego, Cal. Coldest Day on Record" at 22 degrees Fahrenheit on January 7, 1913. It was so cold that the water in the Horton Plaza Fountain froze, and crowds gathered to witness the sight. A sign on the corner of the Brick Block reads, "this building will be remodeled," and there is a Stanley Model 810 Mountain Climber (c. 1913) parked in front of the U.S. Grant Hotel advertising round-trip passage from San Diego to Tijuana–Old Mexico for $1 per person. (SDHC.)

Rev. Lincoln A. Ferris served as minister from 1917 to 1924. Reverend Ferris was an articulate speaker. During his ministry, the idea was conceived to have a Methodist Camp for the young people and adult groups for weekend outings and religious meetings. The church leased land on Mt. Laguna from the government for this purpose.

This c. 1918 photograph shows dozens of soldiers, sailors, and marines assembled with members of the congregation in front of the Ninth and C Street church after a Sunday worship service. (SDHC.)

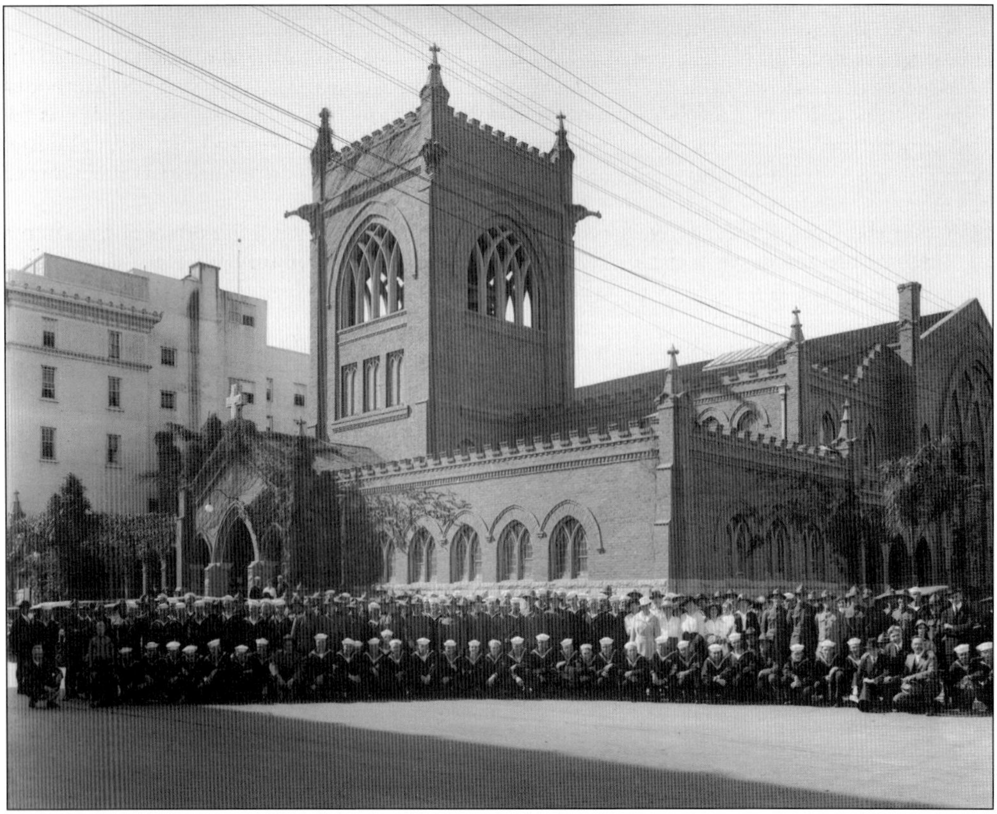

Four

GROWTH AND RENOVATIONS
CHANGES AT NINTH AND C STREETS
(1918–1958)

From 1924 through 1935, throughout the first part of the Great Depression, First Methodist was led by Rev. Dr. Frank Linder. In May 1918, an electric cross donated by Frank and Georgia Lynch was mounted on top of the bell tower. Dr. Linder started calling First Methodist the "Church of the Cross, the Chimes and the Crowds" after he observed the revolving cross, heard the Hartupee chimes, and met the increasing numbers of new members. First Church became a fixture of San Diego with its lighted cross tower and its bells ringing out to the ocean.

During a remodeling of the church exterior in the early 1940s, the gargoyles that had graced the bell tower since 1907 were removed. Rev. Dr. Walter John Sherman was pastor of First Methodist Church from 1935 to 1939. This was in the latter part of the Great Depression, which was felt throughout the country. In 1939 Dr. Sherman experienced a stroke, and his pastoral duties were carried forward by an associate pastor until Rev. Dr. George A. Warmer was appointed minister.

During the years of the two world wars (1914–1917 and 1939–1945), the doors of the church were open seven days a week, providing many services for lonely military members who were far from home. It was said that sailors at sea would hear the chimes from First Church and know that they were almost home.

It was during the ministries of Dr. Warmer (1940–1948) and Rev. Dr. Stanley S. McKee (1948–1958) that several renovations, including a remodeled sanctuary and converting a patio area into a chapel, were completed. In 1940, the address of the Ninth and C Street location was changed. The new street number was selected by a church secretary. The original address was 845 C Street, and the new address was 1112 Ninth Street. In the 1950s, even with renovations and additions, First Church recognized that the congregation was outgrowing its facilities and the site did not have adequate parking.

Dr. McKee guided the search for a new location. Ten and a half acres were purchased in the heart of rural Mission Valley for $160,000. Rev. Dr. Noel C. LeRoque came to First Methodist Church in 1958, and his focus was keeping the church at Ninth and C Streets flourishing until the congregation moved to Mission Valley.

In 1918, a revolving illuminated cross was added to the tower at the Ninth and C Street church. The cross was a gift from Frank and Georgia Lynch. This c. 1920 photograph shows the church with the new cross. When Dr. Frank Linder became minister in 1924, he asked the church's board to adopt the slogan: "The Church of the Cross, the Chimes, and the Crowds." (SDHC.)

Rev. Dr. Frank Linder served as First Church's pastor from 1924 to 1935. According to *Landmark of a Century*, published in 1969, Dr. Linder recalled the Ninth and C Street church as a "very useful building with superior acoustics—he never had to use sound equipment— and a seating capacity of 1,400."

The church choir is pictured here in front of the church around 1925. The first robes were worn by the choir in 1910. During the 1920s, the lighted revolving cross and the chimes were already in existence, and Dr. Linder had complete faith that the "crowds" would soon be there to fulfill the promise of his slogan.

The Ninth and C Street church is pictured on Easter Sunday, April 20, 1930. According to a note on the back of the photograph, the sanctuary was decorated with spring flowers, including a cross made of Easter lilies, by Lydah Linder, the pastor's wife.

Celebrations were planned and carried out for the 70th anniversary of the church in 1939. According to *Landmark of the Century*, a housewarming was held Sunday through Wednesday of the anniversary week. A pageant presented the church's history with a look forward to 1940 and a look backward to 1869. This 1939 photograph shows members on the church steps at the C Street entrance.

Rev. Walter John Sherman served as the pastor at First Church from 1935 to 1940. During the Great Depression, ministers and laymen alike felt insecure, since it was a difficult time for churches to fund their budgets.

The interior of the church at Ninth and C Streets is shown on Easter Sunday, April 12, 1936, before it was remodeled.

The patio area on C Street was located to the west of the church's main entrance. This 1940s image is one of the few known photographs that shows how the inside of the patio looked before the Lynch Memorial Chapel was built in 1950.

Rev. Dr. George A. Warmer served as the pastor at First Methodist from 1940 to 1948. As minister in a downtown church during wartime, Dr. Warmer provided a homelike atmosphere. He was present at the church from morning until late at night, seven days a week, and was always available to give communion, to counsel, to perform marriages, and to offer cordial fellowship.

This photograph was taken on Easter Sunday, April 25, 1943, after the chancel and altar area at the Ninth and C Street church were remodeled with golden oak paneling. Rev. Russell Bales, assistant pastor (left), and Rev. Dr. George A. Warmer, lead pastor, are shown here.

Marie Fowler, pictured in 1943, served as the Fellowship Lounge hostess at the Ninth and C Street church. She oversaw the lounge and other activities at First Church from the fall of 1942 through 1947. The lounge was sometimes called "the Home Away from Home." Thousands visited and knew that wherever they were on the face of the earth, there was a group of people remembering them in prayer.

The Fellowship Lounge was in a small parlor at the southwest corner of the Ninth and C Street church. The lounge was a popular place for members of the armed forces to gather in the afternoons and evenings to play games, socialize, and enjoy refreshments. This c. 1943 photograph shows the lounge's interior as it appeared during World War II—although it was usually occupied by service members.

In the early 1940s, the gargoyles that had graced the bell tower since 1907 were removed during a general remodeling of the church. In December 1941, the church's building superintendent, Walter E. Knouse, discovered that the main supporting beams of the church were out of line. A plan for renovation, redecoration, and beautification was completed in 1943. This c. 1943 photograph shows the completed modern exterior. (SDHC.)

Taken in 1944 at the Ninth and C Street church on the Sunday preceding the 75th anniversary of Methodism in San Diego, this photograph shows people who were members and/or attended when the church worshipped in the Brick Block at Fourth Street and D Street (now Broadway) when it moved in 1907.

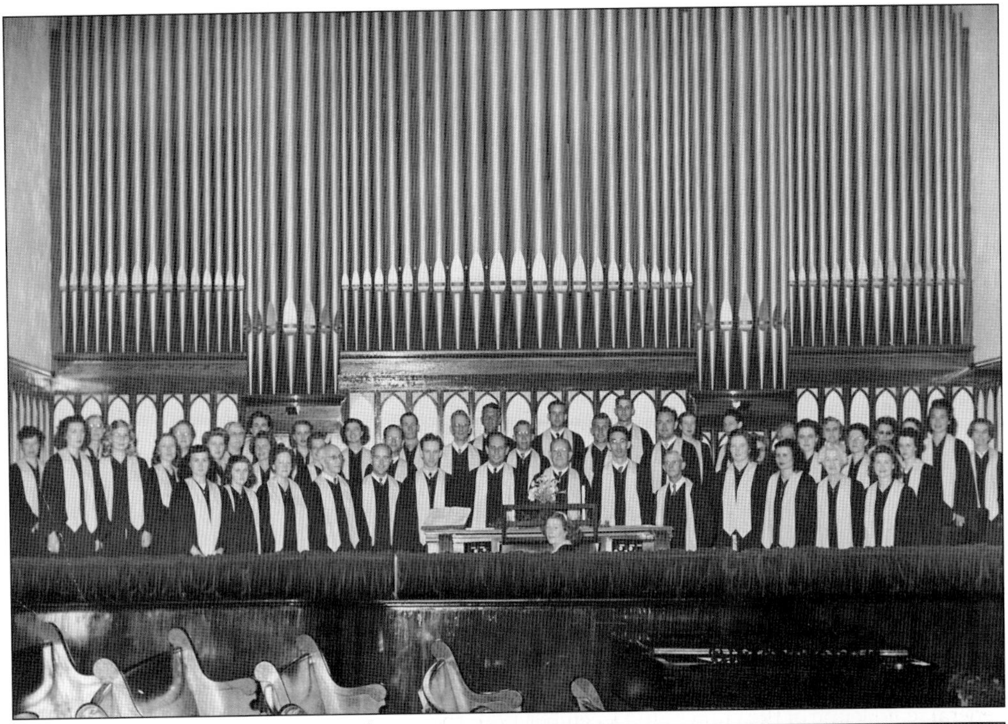

The church choir is shown around 1946 in the choir loft in front of the 27-rank, three-manual Pilcher pipe organ that was dedicated in 1929. This organ included 1,877 pipes with harp and chimes.

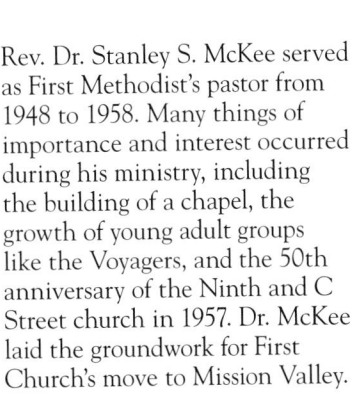

Rev. Dr. Stanley S. McKee served as First Methodist's pastor from 1948 to 1958. Many things of importance and interest occurred during his ministry, including the building of a chapel, the growth of young adult groups like the Voyagers, and the 50th anniversary of the Ninth and C Street church in 1957. Dr. McKee laid the groundwork for First Church's move to Mission Valley.

The 1948 view above of the Ninth and C Street church shows C Street looking northeast, while the image below, also taken around 1948, looks northwest from Ninth Street. These amateur photographs were discovered in First Church's time capsule, located on the current Mission Valley site and opened in November 2014 for the Crossroads Celebration of 50 years at Mission Valley.

Around 1947, Dr. George A. Warmer arranged to end the lease of the church's camp at Mt. Laguna when he learned that First Church could buy Cornell Ranch, northeast of Julian. Much work and many years of volunteer service were required to make the property usable. The renamed ranch, Cedar Glen, was given as a gift to the Southern California Methodist Conference. This c. 1949 photograph shows the Voyagers group in front of Cedar Glen's newly painted dining hall.

The revolving illuminated cross atop the tower was added in 1918. This late 1940s postcard image shows the exterior remodeling that included the removal of the gargoyles. During World War II, the church's cross and bell tower went dark during the blackouts that were enforced along both the East and West Coasts. From very shortly after Pearl Harbor until early in 1945, the revolving cross was not visible at night.

Sunday school classes have been a source of faith formation in the Methodist church through the years. This 1950s photograph shows a gathering of school-aged children in the basement at the Ninth and C Street church.

The Ninth and C Street church basement was also used for social events. This photograph is from the Mother/Daughter Banquet held in 1953. (Bruce and Cheryl Johnson.)

The church at Ninth and C Streets includes the Georgia Lynch Memorial Chapel and classrooms above it, which were dedicated on March 26, 1950. The chapel was built over the patio area on C Street to the west of the church's main entrance. The windblown patio was commonly filled with papers from the street. A second story built above the chapel included five classrooms.

From the late 1940s to early 1950, additions to the Ninth and C Street church included Sunday school rooms and a chapel. The chapel was a gift from the Lynch Family Trust and was named the Georgia Lynch Memorial Chapel. It was a popular location for prayer services and small weddings.

The Challengers group, formerly called the Young Married Class, was established in 1936. This photograph was taken in 1956 at a party to celebrate the Challengers' 20th year in existence. Members pictured here are, from left to right, (first row) Walt and Vera Dermeyer, Lois Johnson, Mary Astley, Dick Johnson, Ethyl Harter, and Marjorie and Ed Eagle; (second row) Frank and Lucille Wherry, Emil and Romona Johnson, Frank Astley, and Dick Harter. (Bruce and Cheryl Johnson.)

This photograph shows the Methodist congregation in April 1957 during a Good Friday service at the Ninth and C Street church. This image, taken from the sanctuary's balcony, is one of the few in the church archives taken during a church service and showing the general layout of the Ninth and C Street sanctuary.

A group of
unidentified Sunday
school students
at the Ninth and
C Street location
are pictured with
teacher Paul Jones
around 1958.

Stories and scriptures from the Bible are the focus of Sunday school classes like this c. 1958 one at the Ninth and C Street church location.

This c. 1950 picture shows the Ninth and C Street church looking southwest from the corner of Ninth and B Streets. The Hotel Churchill building, which was erected in 1914 to house visitors attending the Panama-California Exposition, is visible in the background. From the 1940s to the 1950s, the coffee shop at the Hotel Churchill was a popular gathering place after church.

Five

SITE AND FORESIGHT
MISSION VALLEY ACCOMPLISHED
(1958–1964)

Around 1957, construction began on the US 80 freeway (renamed Interstate 8) between US 395 (renamed California 163), Ward Road (the future Interstate 15), and Mission Gorge Road. When the Mission Valley land was purchased in 1958, San Diego's center was moving outward, which was why First Church looked beyond downtown for its new home.

This move was perhaps one of the most courageous acts of faith in the church's history. In the mid-1950s, there were no large buildings on the floor of Mission Valley, which flooded at times during the rainy seasons. Dairy farms and cornfields dotted the rural landscape. Yet, studies predicting the city's growth indicated that Mission Valley would be the population center within a decade. The church chose an L-shaped, 10.5-acre location at the crossroads of the new interstate system.

Following the purchase, families and church groups picnicked on the beautiful slope and dreamed of the church they would someday build there. However, Rev. Dr. Noel C. LeRoque, minister from 1958 to 1965, was a man of action. The focus of his ministry was to convert dreams into reality and move First Church to the new site. The task of building a "cathedral-style" sanctuary began in 1960, when Reginald Inwood of Laguna Beach was selected as the architect. His Spanish Contemporary design reflects the history of Mission Valley, where the Franciscan Fathers built San Diego de Alcala, the first California mission, in 1769.

When the land was purchased, the premises had a ranch house and barn. The Voyagers, one of the adult Sunday school groups, tore down the barn. Other groups, including the Challengers, renovated the ranch house so that it could be used for work parties and other events. The land was cleared and graded, making it usable so people could drive to the top and have a better look at the area.

The ground-breaking ceremony for the Mission Valley church took place on August 11, 1963, after Sunday services at the Ninth and C Street church, and included at least 550 people in attendance. The address of the Mission Valley location is 2111 Camino del Rio South, which is the numerical inverse of the 1112 Ninth Street address. No documentation has been found in the church archives about whether this reversal of address numbers was a deliberate choice or purely a coincidence. On November 8, 1964, the first church service was held in Mission Valley.

The land for the new location was purchased in 1958. The ranch house, shed, and barn in the lower left corner were on the church site when it was purchased. One of the church's adult Sunday school classes, the Voyagers, tore down the barn, while other church groups, including the Challengers, renovated the ranch house. This c. 1958 view looks east toward Texas Street and where the San Diego Stadium was located.

Rev. Dr. Noel C. LeRoque served as the pastor from 1958 to 1965. His major effort during his ministry at First Church was building and moving into the new Mission Valley location. Dr. LeRoque recalled in *Landmark of the Century*, "Our major concern at first, was keeping the church at Ninth and C Streets alive until the building program could be carried out."

This 1961 view of Mission Valley looks east. First Church chose a location at the crossroads of the new interstate system. (SDHC.)

The breaking of ground on the Mission Valley site took place on August 11, 1963. After Sunday services, members caravanned from the Ninth and C Street church for the special ceremony. At least 550 people were on hand. (SDHC.)

Excavation for the Mission Valley church began in August 1963. This view of the site from that year looks northeast toward Interstate 8 and Texas Street.

Excavation continued in late summer 1963. This view of the site looks northwest toward Interstate 8 and the Mission Valley Mall, which opened in 1961.

Looking west across the Mission Valley location, excavation of the sanctuary basement is visible in this 1963 view. The Mission Valley Mall is to the right in the background.

The construction of the basement below the sanctuary is shown in this 1963 photograph looking northwest on Mission Valley. The Sentinel Savings and May Co. Auto Center buildings, both of which are no longer standing, are visible across Interstate 8.

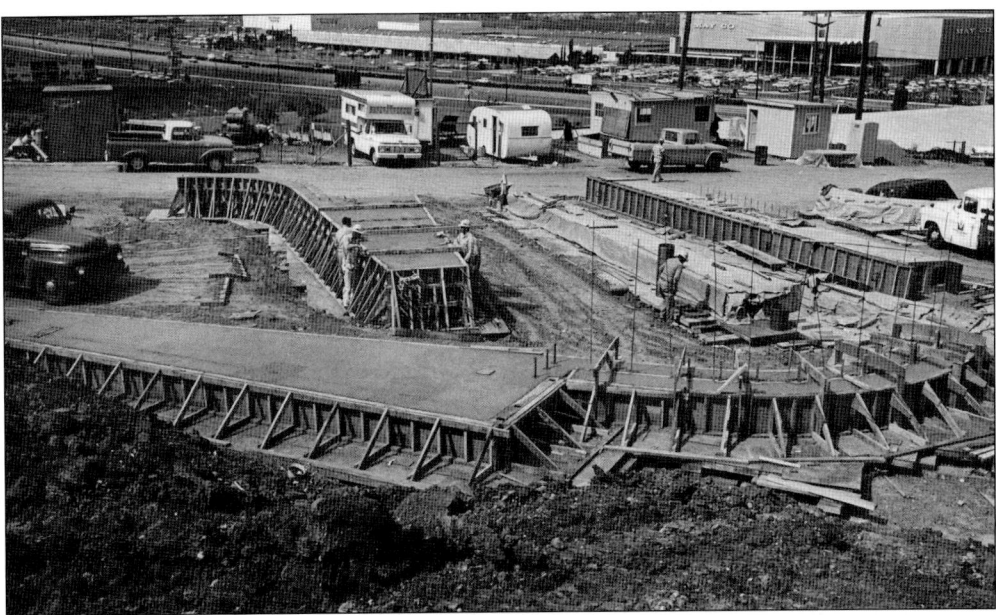

The forms for the sanctuary columns under construction in the basement area at the Mission Valley location are visible in this 1963 view looking northeast.

The concrete finishing on the main arches are pictured here around 1963.

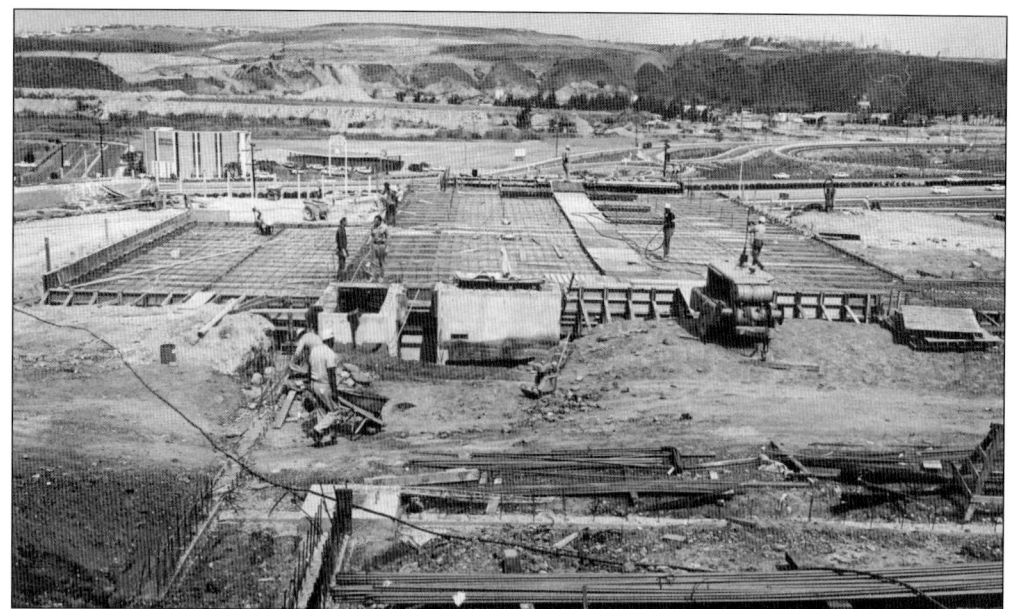

The sanctuary's foundation steel is tied and ready for concrete to be poured in this 1963 picture.

The flooring of the sanctuary is being lowered into place. This 1963 photograph is looking north with a view of the hills beyond Mission Valley.

Construction of the Mission Valley location cost $1.6 million. This 1963 photograph shows some of the precast concrete forms that were poured on-site. The May Co. department store at Mission Valley Mall is visible on the right, across Interstate 8.

When the Mission Valley sanctuary of First Church was built during 1963 and 1964, it was considered the largest use of standing, or "tilt-up," precast concrete on the West Coast.

This is a 1964 view of the sanctuary from the back looking south toward the future location of the chancel, altar, and large glass window. Nearly all of the arches are up, and the ceiling of the sanctuary nave measures 65 feet above ground level, which is evident when compared to the construction worker in this photograph. The central nave of the sanctuary is 150 feet long.

By March 1964, the construction theme was "Raise the Arches for Easter." The biggest tilt-up job for precast concrete yet attempted on the West Coast began that month as arches were raised to form the sanctuary of First Methodist Church in Mission Valley. For several months, the Golden Construction Company cast arches and girders on the site.

This aerial view looks south on First Methodist Church as construction continued in 1964. The sanctuary's main arches are in place, and the auxiliary buildings of the church campus (for an office and Sunday school classrooms) are completed. Interstate 8 is in the foreground and Texas Street is to the east (left).

The construction crew lowered the cement pieces of the tracery window frames into place section by section with the help of a crane.

Each section of tracery windows was capped at the top of the arch before the roof could be put in place in 1964. The 18 tracery windows that line the arch of the sanctuary are 14 feet wide by 30 feet high and weigh 12 tons each.

After all the tracery window frames were in place, construction moved to completing the front section of the church sanctuary in 1964. The circular stairways at lower left were not yet enclosed.

In the foreground of this 1964 picture is one of the nearly completed Sunday school buildings with the Mission Valley sanctuary taking shape beyond it.

By the second half of 1964, the sanctuary was nearly done. Before the cross was put in place, a construction worker apparently took a giant piece of red-painted plywood and fashioned a "flag" for the new edifice. Through the years, the cathedral church has been affectionately referred to as "The Mailbox" by some San Diegans. This photograph shows the front interior circular stairways enclosed, the gunite shell roof installed, and the exterior being painted.

This 1964 photograph of the interior of the Mission Valley sanctuary shows some of the scaffolding and support frames that were necessary to complete the walls and roof. In this picture, looking south, the front glass windows have not yet been installed.

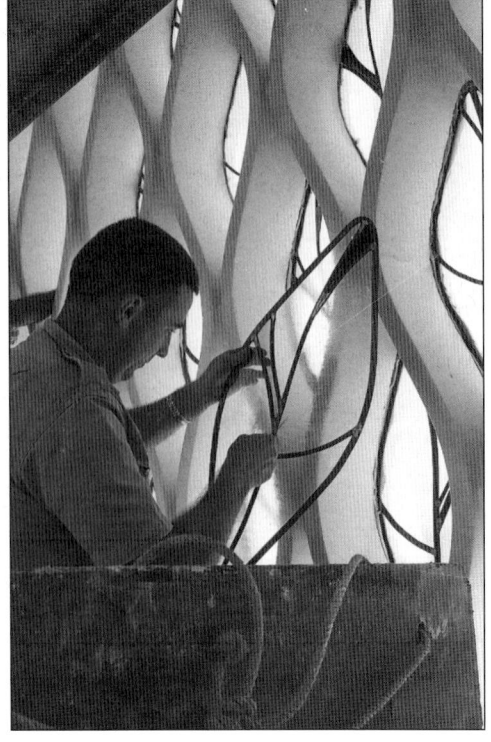

In autumn 1964, the tracery's stained-glass windows were individually installed. The honeycomb design symbolizes the flow of the River of Life, with the stained glass illustrating the vines and leaves of the Tree of Life. The colors of the stained glass are in shades of yellow, orange, and red that grow from a simple to complex pattern. In the late afternoon, the west-facing windows produce a sunset-like glow that blankets the sanctuary.

The completed buildings of the Mission Valley church location are shown here in autumn 1964. Note the lack of landscaping, barren hillside, and no cross (yet). The church sanctuary was built on a base in the shape of a cross, 150 feet long and 65 feet wide. The arches and beams support 137 tons of gunite shell and precast tracery windows.

This September 1964 picture of the nearly completed Mission Valley church site was taken from the main driveway off Camino del Rio South.

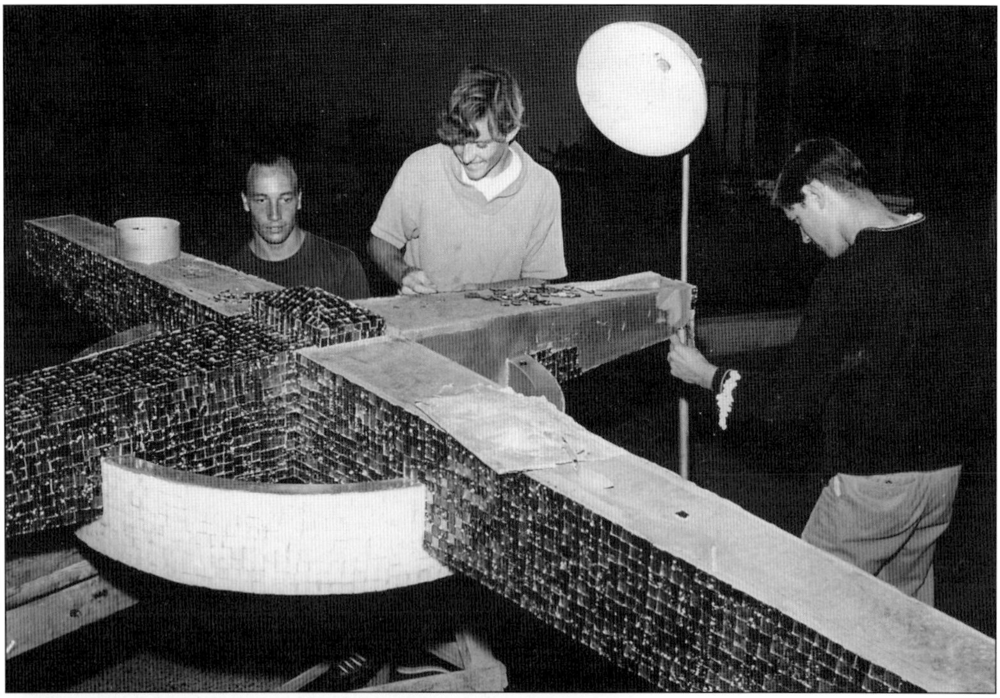

The eight-foot cross on top of the Mission Valley sanctuary is made of steel and adorned with copper and gold mosaic glass. This October 1964 photograph shows the "night crew" tiling the cross.

In October 1964, the glistening eight-foot cross was installed on a 32-foot steel needle atop the sanctuary.

A giant crane was used to place the cross, made of steel and mosaic glass tiles, high above the sanctuary.

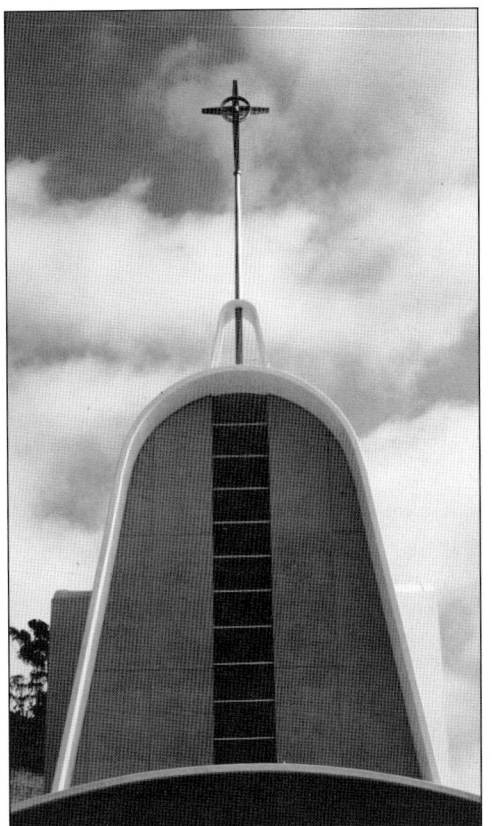

By the time the cross was installed and the sanctuary almost completed, people from the congregation and community were making special trips up and down the freeway to have a look at the new edifice in Mission Valley. Many were attracted to the property for a closer look.

In September 1964, work crews put the finishing touches on the new $1,600,000 Mission Valley landmark, First Methodist Church. In late October, the church was ready for the big transition from Ninth and C Street to Mission Valley.

The next step was to move the church equipment from the Ninth and C Street property to the congregation's new home. The completed Mission Valley site is pictured in early November 1964.

Six

MOVING DAYS
CATHEDRAL CHURCH AT THE INTERCHANGE
(1964–1969)

The "cathedral-style" church seats 1,100 people and is built on a base in the shape of a cross—200 feet long and 65 feet wide. The nave is 65 feet high, and the circular stairs in the foyer rise to 75 feet. The four 74-ton support beams were cast on-site, and a 90-ton crane was used to raise them into place. The 18 tracery windows that line the arch of the sanctuary are 14 feet wide by 30 feet high and each weigh 12 tons. These windows, combined with the huge gunite sanctuary shell, place a weight of 137 tons on the support beams. High above the church, mounted upon a 32-foot needle of steel, is the eight-foot cross made of steel and gold mosaic glass tiles.

The altar and chancel offer worshippers a view of the sanctuary garden behind floor-to-ceiling windows. The terrazzo floor of the chancel holds a medallion in the shape of a cross with symbols of the four Gospels—an angel for Matthew, a winged lion for Mark, a winged ox for Luke, and an eagle for John. The Twelve Apostles Altar is made of white mosaic with three-foot-tall figures of the disciples. The cross has a dove at the center representing the Holy Spirit. Beautiful kneeling pads depicting scriptural phrases were made by church members. More than 30 people, ranging in age from 12 to 80, handcrafted the needlepoint cushions for the kneeling rail of the altar. A mosaic of John Wesley, the father of Methodism, is depicted on the pulpit with his words, "I look upon all the world as my parish," and the lectern holds the eagle of the Gospel of John. On November 22, 1964, the Mission Valley sanctuary was consecrated.

Relocating the church was not without crisis, even after the move. There was a concern about whether First Church could carry the financial load, and attendance was not good in late 1965. However, the predictions of growth began to materialize, and membership at the church increased under the leadership of Rev. C.A. McClain, who served from 1965 to 1976. First Church began to take on different characteristics. Young adults with children found the new church campus and ministry to be of great value to them. Early in 1968, a committee was formed to plan the year-long celebration for the 100th anniversary of Methodism in San Diego that would occur in 1969.

Pictured here is a Good Friday worship service at the Ninth and C Street church on March 27, 1964. This photograph is one of the few that show the sanctuary from the balcony. Across town, the Mission Valley site was under construction at this time. (SDHC.)

The wedding of Nancy Goslow and Lawrence (Larry) Wherry, held on June 13, 1964, was one of the final marriage ceremonies at the Ninth and C Street sanctuary. The minister who officiated was Rev. Hilka Green. The maid of honor was Gerrie Trewella, and the best man was John Hermann. (Wherry family.)

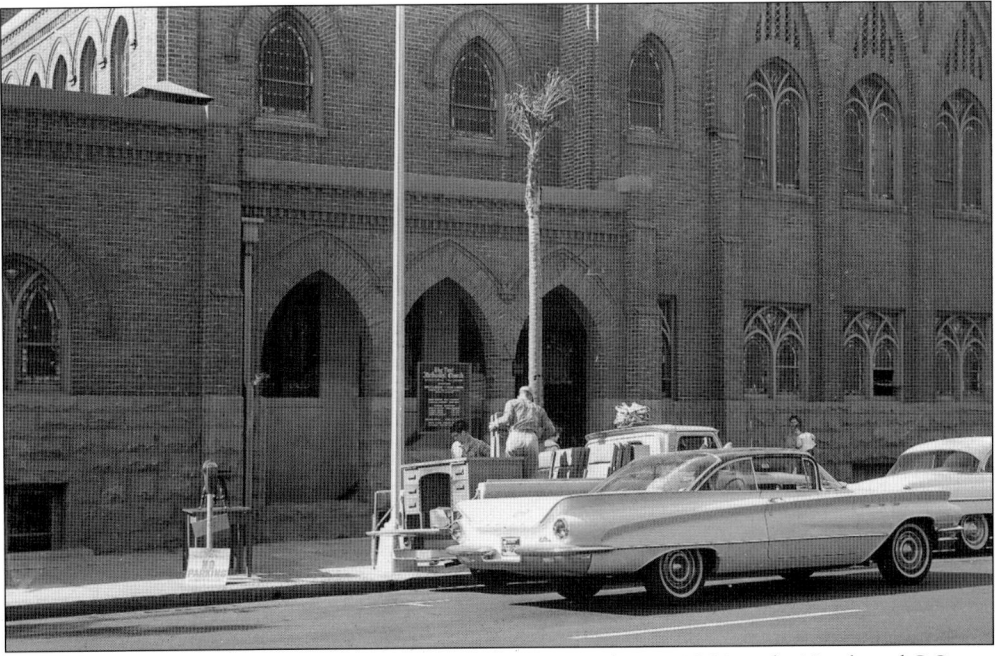

As the congregation was anticipating its move to Mission Valley, the location at Ninth and C Streets was put up for sale. This 1964 photograph shows the church with a "For Sale" sign on the corner of the building above the marquee. (SDHC.)

Nearly 100 volunteer workers assembled at 8:00 a.m. on October 31, 1964, at the Ninth and C Street property to move the church equipment to the congregation's new home in Mission Valley.

The volunteer movers manned a dozen pickup trucks, trailers, station wagons, and cars hauling office equipment, tables, chairs, books, nursery equipment, and other furnishings to the new sanctuary and auxiliary buildings at 2111 Camino del Rio in Mission Valley.

The moving project was completed on November 1, 1964, after the final morning service in the Ninth and C Street church. This photograph shows the altar and chancel furniture being prepared for the move.

After all of the church furnishings were moved, a vesper service was held in the new Mission Valley church at 6:00 p.m. for those who helped with moving, and others who wished to come. Not all of the chancel furnishings were in, nor were the pews. Folding chairs were rented to provide sufficient seating.

Walter Knouse, carillonneur, played a final program before the bells, which had rung out over the city since 1908, were dismantled and moved to storage in Mission Valley. This last playing of the chimes was recorded so the hymns could be played at the new church until the bell tower could be funded and built. This November 1964 photograph shows the chiming stand console inside the Ninth and C Street bell tower. (SDHC.)

The Mission Valley sanctuary and the surrounding area are shown in this 1964 picture taken from the end of Lomitas Drive looking north.

This is a 1964 view of the sanctuary and west transept. A parking lot was also located on this side adjacent to the transept doors.

The interior of the Mission Valley sanctuary is pictured in 1964. The first service was held on November 8, 1964, and the consecration service took place on November 22, 1964. The three large olive trees outside the sanctuary window were donated by Mr. and Mrs. Berma Bonham and Mr. and Mrs. Harley Bonham. Berma and Harley Bonham owned Bonham Brothers Mortuary and established the Bonham Brothers Band in 1926.

A parking lot was located directly outside the transept doors, as shown in this 1964 photograph of the sanctuary and east transept at Mission Valley church.

This 1964 nighttime photograph of the completed sanctuary taken from the hillside looks through the floor-to-ceiling windows behind the altar. The ceiling of the nave rises 65 feet above ground level, and the central nave of the sanctuary is 150 feet long.

A mosaic of John Wesley, the father of Methodism, is depicted on the pulpit along with his words, "I look upon all the world as my parish." This photograph shows a close-up of the mosaic.

All of the items on the altar were designed by Reginald Inwood and brought to life by two California artists, Alan Pendergast and Joseph McShane. The main sections of the altar are white mosaic with three-foot-tall figures of the disciples and the cross with a dove at the center representing the Holy Spirit.

The sanctuary altar depicts the 12 apostles at the Last Supper. It is made of more than 100 different colors of mosaic tile. This close-up shows St. James, who has the most prominent position in the design, and St. John, who is shown with a communion cup.

Rev. Dr. Noel C. LeRoque, shown in the foyer of the sanctuary inside the front doors at the plaza level, visits with church members following a worship service in 1964.

The lectern holds a mosaic eagle representing the Gospel of John.

In 1965, one year after construction of the Mission Valley sanctuary was completed, some landscaping was completed. The congregation celebrated the first anniversary of the new church with a fellowship dinner held at the Scottish Rite Masonic Memorial Center next door to the church, with 700 people in attendance.

In July 1964, escrow closed on the sale of the Ninth and C Street church property when it was purchased by A.W. Coggeshall. This c. 1965 photograph shows the dismantling and demolition in progress. In the downtown area, it was expected that the land would be developed with commercial structures after the building was removed. However, as of 2018, the land has remained in use as a parking lot. (SDHC.)

Rev. C.A. McClain Jr. served as First Church's senior pastor from 1965 to 1976 and was known for his far-reaching, thought-provoking sermons. Reverend McClain emphasized the solvency of the church and urged members "to lift according to their strength." The monthly mortgage payments were met, and new programs were formulated.

A highlight of the fellowship dinner, held to celebrate the church's first anniversary in Mission Valley, was the opening of the Cornerstone Box that had been sealed in the Ninth and C Street church cornerstone in 1906. According to *Landmark of the Century*, two San Diego women, Lillian Works and Carrie Weckerly, who had seen the box dedicated in 1906, assisted with the opening of it.

In November 1965, the Cornerstone Box arrived at the Mission Valley site in a 1910 Buick driven by Bill Evans. This photograph shows the congregation gathering around the automobile in the plaza area outside the sanctuary.

The Mission Valley church interior is shown here around 1967. This photograph shows how the chancel looked before the low wall was installed in front of the choir pews.

When the church was first used for worship services in early November 1964, not all of the chancel furnishings were in—including the "white Naugahyde" pews. Folding chairs were rented to provide sufficient seating for the first few months. In 1964, the sanctuary carpet was a golden yellow color, the north window was clear glass, and the pipe organ was not the same one in the gallery today. This photograph (date unknown) shows the completed interior of the Mission Valley sanctuary with the pews in place.

The centennial year celebrations began on December 27, 1968, when Duke Ellington and his orchestra presented "A Sacred Concert" at the Mission Valley sanctuary.

A Centennial Event

DUKE ELLINGTON

AND HIS ORCHESTRA

present

A SACRED CONCERT

DECEMBER 27, 1968
8:00 P.M.

SANCTUARY CHOIR

First United Methodist Church
OF SAN DIEGO
2111 Camino del Rio (Mission Valley)
SAN DIEGO, CALIFORNIA

MINISTERS
C. A. McCLAIN, JR.   HILKA D. GREEN

Rev. C.A. McClain and Duke Ellington are pictured on November 21, 1970, at the Cocoanut Grove in Los Angeles. They met to finalize plans for "Sacred Jazz Concert," a follow-up to the centennial event held in December 1968.

The services on Christmas Eve in 1969 included a candle-lighting ceremony led by some of the young women of First Church. (SDHC.)

Seven

CELEBRATIONS AND CHANGES
BUILDING ON THE DREAM
(1969–PRESENT)

In 1964, when the Mission Valley sanctuary was dedicated, the plans for a bell tower, a fellowship hall, and a chapel were put on hold. These dreams and more have become reality through the years. The bell tower was completed on the hill overlooking the valley in 1976. It contains the 11 original Hartupee chimes, which were cast in 1907, from the old downtown church at Ninth and C Street. The bells weigh 9,600 pounds and can be played from the organ console. In 1983, Linder Hall—a multipurpose building with administrative offices, conference rooms, and the social hall—was dedicated. The 23,000-square-foot structure was built under the leadership of Rev. Mark Trotter, minister from 1976 to 2000.

The sanctuary was thoroughly renovated from 1987 to 1988. During that time, the memorial stained glass was installed in the north window of the sanctuary. It stands 42 feet high and portrays the Tree of Life. The sanctuary pipe organ is essentially two instruments located in the chancel and gallery. The original gallery organ was the 27-rank Pilcher organ installed at the Ninth and C Street church in 1928. It was later removed, rebuilt, and enlarged to 40 ranks in 1967. The most recent renovation, in the late 1980s, greatly enhanced the organ. There are now over 6,000 pipes, arranged in 107 ranks, with three 32-foot ranks and a set of stunning cornets. The longest pipe is approximately 32 feet long. It is one of the grandest organs on the West Coast and was dedicated in 1989.

Rev. Dr. Jim Standiford served as senior minister from 2000 to 2013. In 2009, First Church celebrated its 140th anniversary with celebrations that included a special worship service and a picnic. The Trotter Chapel and Music Building, named after Reverend Trotter, was completed in 2006 and completed the church campus as it was originally planned when the congregation moved to Mission Valley.

From 2013 to 2018, Rev. Craig Brown served as the congregation's lead pastor. Under his leadership, and through a transition year guided by Rev. Melissa Spence, First Church incorporated the congregation formerly known as Point Loma United Methodist Church (PLUM), to become a "multi-site congregation." In 2018, Rev. Jessica Strysko led the worshipping community known as the Water's Edge from its home in Mission Valley to the PLUM facilities in Ocean Beach.

First United Methodist Church of San Diego planned a year-long celebration in 1969 to honor the church's centennial.

This 1970 postcard image shows the First United Methodist Church of San Diego in Mission Valley. The contemporary Spanish architecture reflects the history of Mission Valley, where the Franciscans built the first California mission, San Diego de Alcala, in 1769.

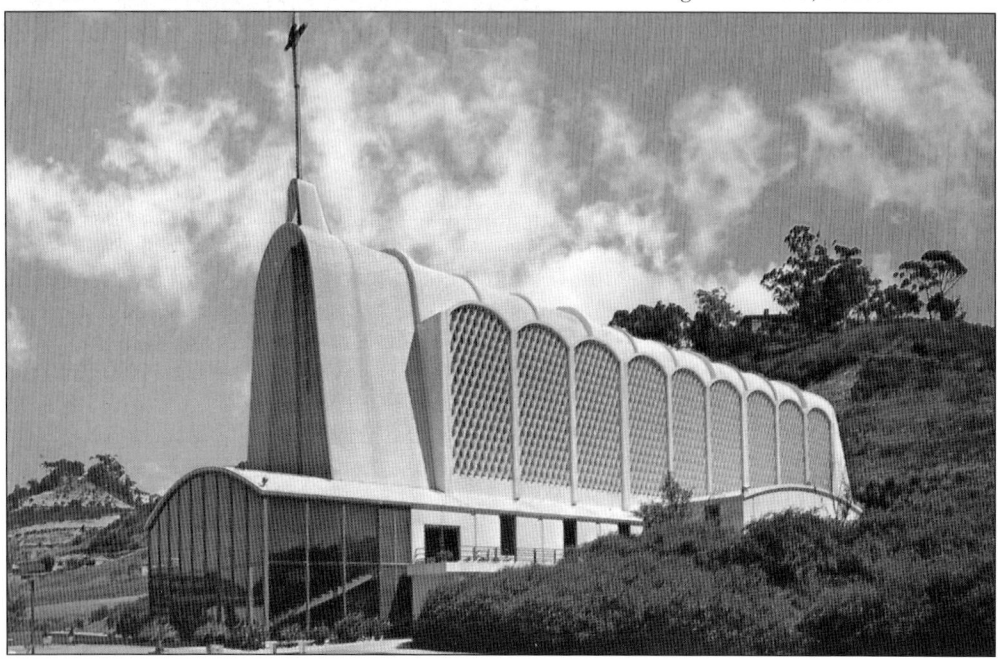

A group of youth from the United Methodist Youth Fellowship (UMYF) of First Church pose on September 23, 1973, at the top of Mt. Whitney (14,505 feet), the tallest mountain in California. Mt. Whitney is also the highest summit in the contiguous United States and in the Sierra Nevada mountain range.

Michelle Lambert, with other youth from First United Methodist in the procession behind her, is shown lighting her candle during the Christmas Eve candle-lighting ceremony at First Church in 1973. (SDHC.)

After being silent for 12 years, the 11 bronze bells kept in storage at First Church played again at Fourth of July services in 1976, and the Memorial Bell Tower was dedicated. This photograph shows the bell tower under construction on the hillside above the sanctuary. Bells around the country chimed in unison to celebrate the bicentennial of the United States, and the Hartupee chimes participated. They were once again enjoyed by the people of San Diego. (SDHC.)

This photograph shows unidentified women looking at one of the bells in 1976. The bells were put away when First Church moved in 1964, since no money was available to include a bell tower in original construction plans. The bells were green with age, but the inscriptions were still readable.

Rev. Mark Trotter served as First Church's senior minister from 1976 to 2000. His inspiring preaching ministry drew crowds to three Sunday morning services each week. Under the leadership of Reverend Trotter, Linder Hall was built, the church sanctuary was renovated, and the "Tree of Life" stained-glass window was installed.

The lower level of the Mission Valley site became an ideal location for a car-wash fundraiser. This 1977 photograph shows members of the UMYF taking part in a car wash.

This is a 1978 view of the Mission Valley sanctuary looking northwest. The land to the east of the sanctuary is where Linder Hall is today.

This photograph was taken after a church picnic lunch on the future site of Linder Hall, east of the sanctuary, around 1978. (John Hermann.)

One of the Hartupee chimes is being inspected and prepared for installation in the Memorial Bell Tower around 1979. After being taken out of storage and installed in 1976, the bells were removed and polished before being reinstalled in the renovated tower. This photograph shows the big bell, "Praise," with the dedication engraving: "This beautiful gift of eleven bells was presented by Rev. Gaylord H. Hartupee to the First Methodist Episcopal Church, San Diego, California, March 26, A.D. 1907."

A group of children and women, possibly a preschool or Sunday school class, is pictured here around 1983 walking down a dirt path east of the nearly completed Linder Hall. Today, the path is a paved driveway on the Mission Valley property.

Here is a 1980 view looking east toward Mission Valley. Many changes had occurred with the construction of new businesses and homes since 1958, when First Church chose the location at the crossroads of the interstate system. (SDHC.)

First Church has a long tradition of dedicated stewardship and support for its church family as well as its local, regional, and global communities. This 1984 image shows some unidentified members participating in the United Methodist Mission Walk.

From 1987 to 1988, the sanctuary was thoroughly renovated. This c. 1987 photograph shows how the sanctuary looked before the updates, with the clear glass in the north window and the original gallery organ—the 27-rank 1928 Pilcher organ that had previously been at the Ninth and C Street church.

The memorial stained-glass window was installed in the north window of the sanctuary in 1988. It stands 42 feet high and portrays the Tree of Life, the flames associated with the Pentecost, and a nimbus—the ethereal representation of glory. The sanctuary pipe organ was also greatly enhanced to take advantage of the acoustically brilliant building. The longest pipe is approximately 36 feet long.

The Memorial Garden is located immediately beyond the "Mount of Olives"—the landscaped hill behind the altar window. Along the perimeter of the garden is the columbarium for urns and plaques. The inner wall is designated for wall plaques for honoring or remembering loved ones. The garden was dedicated in 1998. The landscaping of the Memorial Garden creates a pleasant, restful, and quiet area to meditate and reflect.

This c. 2000 Sunday school class is focused on stories and scriptures of the Bible along with arts and crafts activities.

Rev. Dr. Jim Standiford served as First Church's senior minister from 2000 to 2013. Under Dr. Standiford's leadership, the church campus—as it was originally planned when the congregation moved—was completed with the dedication of the chapel and music building.

As Methodists, members agree to be loyal to the church and uphold it by their prayers, their presence, their gifts, and their service. There are many ways that one can serve; one example is volunteering with a Habitat for Humanity work project. This c. 2004 photograph shows a group in front of a completed home.

At the ground-breaking ceremony for the chapel and music building in 2005, the Chancel Choir, directed by Dr. Stanley M. Wicks, performed on risers cut into the dirt on the future site of the music room.

In 2005, construction began on the Trotter Chapel and Sutherland Music Center. This photograph shows the new buildings underway to the west of the Mission Valley Sanctuary.

This 2012 picture of First United Methodist Church of San Diego was taken from across Interstate 8. Over the five decades since this site was completed in 1964, the landscaping has filled in, including deciduous trees that display colorful foliage each autumn.

The completed Trotter Chapel and Sutherland Music Center are shown around 2006. Neil Larson, a church member, was the architect and stated that "this Chapel and Music Center have been designed to lift our awareness to God through prayer and praise, worship, and singing." The consecration service was held on Sunday, May 7, 2006, and marked the completion of the vision of those who moved the church to this location in 1964.

A team of First Church members went to the Atlantic coast region to help with relief efforts after Hurricane Sandy devastated the area in 2012. Sandy was a category 3 storm at its peak and was the deadliest and most destructive hurricane of the 2012 Atlantic hurricane season. This group of church members served for several days, doing general cleanup and making repairs—an example of serving the church, San Diego, and beyond.

First Church youth dressed in costume and held candles as part of this live nativity pageant on Christmas Eve 2013.

Rev. Craig Brown served as First Church's lead pastor from 2013 to 2018. Under his guidance, the church developed and implemented a multiyear strategic plan for growth and became a multisite congregation.

In November 2014, First Church celebrated its 50th anniversary of being located in Mission Valley and also the 145th anniversary of Methodism in San Diego.

In 1979, the Memorial Bell Tower was renovated and dedicated. In the late 1970s, Everett Mehner, a church member, designed, manufactured, and installed the electronic-pneumatic system that permits the bells to be run from the organ console. Previously, the chimes could only be played manually from the 1907 chiming stand that was located beneath the tower. This c. 2014 photograph shows the current appearance of the bell tower at Mission Valley.

This 2001 image offers a view of the interior of the church sanctuary from the chancel looking toward the pews and Tree of Life stained-glass window in the gallery. The terrazzo floor of the chancel holds a medallion in the shape of a cross with the symbols of the four Gospels. (Clifford Weiler.)

Children's choirs have been an integral part of First Church's music program. This c. 2014 photograph shows the children singing in the Mission Valley sanctuary during a Palm Sunday service.

Mission Valley's sanctuary was consecrated on November 22, 1964. In November 2014, a 50th anniversary Crossroads Celebration was held with the theme "Reflect on the Past, Imagine the Future."

First Church has been the venue for countless weddings through the years, including the marriage ceremony of Kristena Clark and Beckett Kirk on August 9, 2014. The Mission Valley sanctuary makes a stunning setting with the landscaped hill behind the altar window. (Beckett and Kristena Kirk.)

Each summer, the Sierra Service Project (SSP) provides opportunities for middle school and high school youth and intergenerational teams to experience the power of serving people from different cultures and backgrounds. The Mission Valley site has hosted SSP groups on occasion. This c. 2014 photograph shows a group, which includes youth from First Church, spelling out "SSP."

Prayers & Squares is an interfaith outreach ministry that combines the gift of prayers with the gift of a handmade quilt. Its purpose is to promote prayer through the use of quilts. This small group, pictured in 2014, meets on a monthly basis to create the quilts.

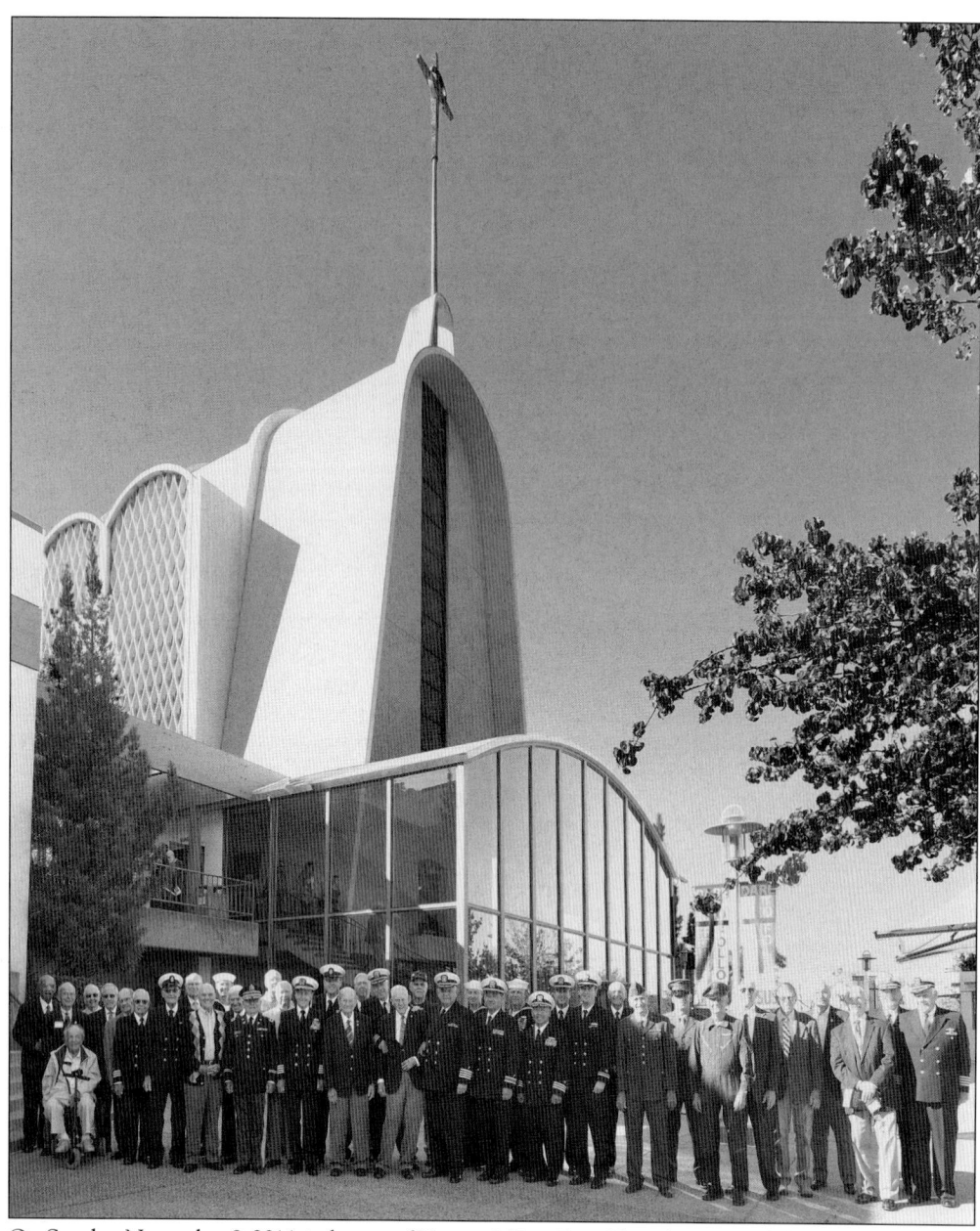

On Sunday, November 9, 2014, in honor of Veteran's Day, First Church recreated the 1918 photograph featured on the cover of this book as part of the Mission Valley site's 50th anniversary celebration. For more than a century, First Church has been a haven for service members, especially during the war years, and it continues to provide a ministry to those who serve our country.

Eight

Point Loma UMC (Ocean Beach)
Merger with First Church

With its own rich history in San Diego, the congregation at Point Loma United Methodist Church (UMC), located in the neighborhood of Ocean Beach, faced a choice of either closing or becoming part of a larger church. Originally established in 1928, Point Loma UMC (PLUM) has seen the Ocean Beach community evolve and change through the years. After serving the people of San Diego for more than eight decades, the members of Point Loma UMC decided a different approach was needed if this congregation was to survive. The California-Pacific Conference of the UMC facilitated discussions with the two congregations, and an official vote was held June 12, 2017, when it was decided that Point Loma UMC would become part of First UMC of San Diego. This chapter includes a few of the photographs from PLUM's history that highlight only some of this church's ministries in Ocean Beach from 1928 to 2017.

In the 1890s, Ocean Beach was a quiet village along the Pacific Ocean. There were a few shacks and frequent picnickers. Around 1907, Ocean Beach was a small community with city water, gas, electricity, and a streetcar line to downtown San Diego.

By the late 1920s, Ocean Beach became a neighborhood of homes, schools, and churches. In April 1928, Point Loma Methodist Church was organized. Less than one year later, in September 1929, the cornerstone was laid for the church sanctuary on Sunset Cliffs Boulevard (formerly Defoe Street). The first church service took place in December 1929, and the official church dedication service was held on February 2, 1930.

In the early 1940s, Ocean Beach was growing into a prosperous village. Along with the community, the Point Loma Methodist congregation was expanding. It was decided that a larger sanctuary should be built to accommodate the membership. In September 1950, construction began on the new sanctuary, and it was completed in March 1951. The original sanctuary, now named Hodge Hall, is used for social and church events.

For the next five decades, PLUM prospered as Ocean Beach became a destination for vacationers and a close-knit community for the San Diegans who call this neighborhood home. In the early 2000s, the number of worshippers began to decline, and the congregation determined that a new path was needed to ensure its survival. After the merger with First UMC of San Diego in 2017, Point Loma UMC was renamed and became a second campus of First Church. The Water's Edge Faith Community, a congregation of First Church, moved from Mission Valley and started worshipping in Ocean Beach in 2018—one church, two campuses. The sanctuary was renovated and Water's Edge is thriving in its new neighborhood—a fitting name for a church campus within blocks of the Pacific Ocean.

After organizing on April 18, 1928, the Point Loma Methodist Church met in various places while raising funds to build a church. From August 1928 through November 1929, the congregation met at the Merry-Go-Round Building that used to be at the foot of Santa Monica Avenue at Abbott Street. From 1918 to 1927, a 1911 Herschell-Spillman carousel was in this building, and when it was moved, the building stayed. It was an Ocean Beach landmark until 1965, when it was torn down. (Ocean Beach Historical Society.)

The church's cornerstone was laid on September 8, 1929, and the new church at 1984 Sunset Cliffs Boulevard was dedicated on February 2, 1930. The cornerstone was opened in March 1978 as part of the church's 50th anniversary to see if there was a time capsule in it. In October 1978, an updated time capsule was placed into the cornerstone, and the mortgage was burned as part of the anniversary celebrations.

This church's original name was the Ocean Beach Community Church. In July 1928, the official name—Point Loma Methodist Episcopal Church—was adopted, and in 1941, the word "Episcopal" was dropped from the name. By the late 1940s, the congregation decided a larger sanctuary was necessary.

This 1947 sketch shows an artist's rendering of the proposed Point Loma Methodist Church sanctuary. The new sanctuary is Mission-style architecture, built of hollow tile brick, and topped with a 60-foot tower. The edifice included a night illumination feature, and the pews and other woodwork were made of mahogany.

Mildred (Millie) Hall and Joseph Earle (Sandy) Sandiford were married on October 2, 1951. Their wedding was the first ceremony held in the new Point Loma Methodist Church sanctuary. They were married by Rev. Paul Beismeier. (Millie Sandiford.)

This December 1960 picture of the courtyard space between the old sanctuary (now known as Hodge Hall), on the right, and the new sanctuary, on the left, looks toward Sunset Cliffs Boulevard. Children are taking part in the Christmas Workshop, which was an ongoing tradition.

In December 1952, Point Loma Methodist hosted a Bible exhibit. This photograph shows John Atwood and Mrs. C.W. Hallar with the Bibles on display in the narthex. (SDHC.)

On December 20, 1958, a living nativity scene with live farm animals was presented in the courtyard of the Point Loma Methodist Church on the corner of Sunset Cliffs Boulevard and Saratoga Avenue to celebrate Christmas. (SDHC.)

In March 1964, Point Loma Methodist hosted a special concert for Easter that featured bell-ringing accompanied by trumpet music. Some special Dutch bells were featured in the concert. In this photograph are, from left to right, Rev. Robert B. Fehlman (holding a trumpet), and Mrs. William Wohlwend and Fran Fehlman. (SDHC.)

This c. 1968 photograph taken inside the sanctuary shows the combined adult, children/youth, and bell choirs at Point Loma Methodist Church.

In 1957, an education building (West Wing) was added to the campus, and in 1966, the sanctuary was remodeled. In 1968, the Methodist churches merged with the Evangelistic United Brethren churches. The church's new name became Point Loma United Methodist Church—fondly known as "PLUM."

The Point Loma United Methodist church courtyard, shown here around 1997, was a popular spot for fellowship after church.

The final church service of the Point Loma United Methodist Church congregation was held on May 28, 2017. This August 2017 photograph shows the inside of the sanctuary looking toward the altar. After the agreement to merge with First UMC of San Diego in June 2017, the Water's Edge congregation from Mission Valley started worshipping in Ocean Beach in 2018.

The mahogany pews from Point Loma United Methodist were sold to make way for a revamped worship space with flexible seating for Water's Edge when the sanctuary was renovated. This August 2017 photograph shows the PLUM sanctuary and balcony before the changes.

Nine

THEN AND NOW
FIRST METHODIST WORSHIP
LOCATIONS IN SAN DIEGO

First United Methodist Church of San Diego has been in mission since 1869. Beginning with the first prayer meeting in February 1869, this church has worshipped in more than seven locations throughout San Diego. As First Church celebrates its 150th year of ministry and service in San Diego, it has two church locations—in Mission Valley and Ocean Beach.

This chapter highlights how the locations where First Church has worshipped appeared then, when the church met there, and how these same locations in San Diego appear now. When the congregation moved from Ninth and C Streets to Mission Valley, several items were brought to the new location. These touchstones have been incorporated into the sanctuary and church campus at the Mission Valley site.

Many changes have occurred at First United Methodist Church of San Diego through the years. Less tangible, but just as important than these material changes, are the influences on the lives touched by the church. Many Methodist pulpits are filled by one-time members of First UMC of San Diego. Missionaries and other leaders call this their home church, not to mention the scores of lay workers trained and inspired for a variety of responsibilities and ministries.

The congregation at First Church knows that people are the heart and soul of a church, and that its mission is to minister to the needs of God's people, to grow in grace, and to reach out in love. The realized vision of a beautiful sanctuary for prayer, worship, and sacrament is a testament to Christ's glory and a beacon of hope for the Kingdom of God on earth.

Imagine if the people who first gathered in 1869 at the candlelight worship and prayer service at the Army barracks could visit San Diego's Methodist churches, and specifically this church, and read its history. They might say, "how far this little candle throws its beams," and they would most certainly rejoice over lighting that candle so long ago.

The US Army barracks built in 1851 were located at H (now Market) and Arctic (now Kettner) Streets. During part of 1869, the barracks were unoccupied by the Army, and the space was used as the meeting place for the first worship service, a prayer meeting, of the Methodist Society on February 6, 1869. This c. 1887 photograph shows the barracks building after it was reoccupied by the Army. It was demolished in 1921 for economic reasons. Today, the location of the barracks has a historical marker in front of Park Place and the Embassy Suites Hotel located at the corner of Kettner Boulevard and N. Harbor Drive. (Above, SDHC.)

The Methodists met on the second floor of Dunham Hall from mid-1869 until moving into their own church building a couple of blocks away in February 1870. It is unknown exactly when or why this building was demolished. The buildings currently located on this section of Fifth Avenue date to the late 1880s. The Llewelyn Building at 722 Fifth Avenue was built in 1887 and is the only French Provincial building in the Gaslamp Quarter. As best as can be determined, the Hopping Pig restaurant, located at 748 Fifth Avenue, is closest to where Dunham Hall was in 1869. (Above, SDHC.)

The M.E. Church Block was a large three-story building on the northeast corner of Fourth and D (now Broadway) Streets. It was dedicated in February 1888 and was the center of San Diego's business community at the start of the 20th century. The c. 1905 photograph above shows the church block with its five-story clock tower, which was a downtown landmark. It also shows the awnings retracted above the doorways. After the Methodists moved to Ninth and C Streets in 1907, the M.E. Church Block was used for various commercial purposes until it was demolished in 1913. The Owl Drug Store building was constructed in its place in 1913 and was used as a department store annex from 1926 to 1936 and again from 1945 to 1970. The c. 1933 photograph below shows the Owl Drug Store with the Holzwasser Department Store, built in 1919, next door. (Below, SDHC.)

Today, both the Holzwasser/Walker Scott and Owl Drug Store buildings are listed in the National Register of Historic Places. The above photograph shows the corner of the U.S. Grant Hotel on the left and the former Owl Drug Store building on the northeast corner of Fourth Street and Broadway. The below photograph shows the renovated Horton Plaza Fountain with the northeast corner of Fourth Street and Broadway in the background. When the Horton Plaza shopping center opened in 1985, the historic park was restored to its 1910 look. In the early 1990s, the park area was removed to discourage homeless campouts, and the fountain, which was a mechanical marvel in its day, stopped working in 2008. Horton Plaza Park was boarded up in 2012 until a complete renovation, which included restoring the fountain to its original glory, was completed in 2016. (Above, SDHC.)

The building designed by Irving J. Gill for the First Methodist Episcopal Church had a Gothic Revival design. The gothic theme was carried into the tower, which was distinguished by four gargoyles, one at each corner. There were some heated discussions during the building of the church concerning the gargoyles. However, Gill declared that they were necessary. The above photograph looks west on C Street and shows the Ninth and C Street church in 1912. The below photograph shows the corner of Ninth and C Streets in June 2018 and also looks west on C Street, with the San Diego Trolley lines in the foreground. The area where the church used to sit is currently a parking lot used by the adjacent companies and the San Diego Symphony. (Above, SDHC.)

The c. 1950 photograph at right shows the Ninth and C Street church looking south from B Street. The Hotel Churchill, built in 1914, is in the background. The below photograph shows the same perspective in June 2018 with the recently remodeled and reopened Hotel Churchill in the background. The Hotel Churchill is an example of how adapting and reusing San Diego's historic buildings makes sense. Even though the church at Ninth and C Streets was not saved from demolition in the 1960s, the Hotel Churchill got a new lease on life when it was acquired and restored by the San Diego Housing Commission as an affordable housing project.

The granite cross that once graced the entrance above the main church entrance on C Street was a gift from James Simpson, who did the stone masonry work. The c. 1911 photograph above shows the Gothic-style church with the gargoyles on the tower. The below photograph shows the granite cross on display at the Mission Valley church site at the plaza level in June 2018. This cross is one of the fixtures from the Ninth and C Street church that was moved and preserved at the Mission Valley location. (Above, SDHC.)

The pews from the Georgia Lynch Memorial Chapel at Ninth and C Streets were moved to the chancel of the sanctuary in Mission Valley and are used by the choir. These pews are another example of an important fixture of the Ninth and C Street church site that was moved and preserved at the Mission Valley location.

When the Georgia Lynch Memorial Chapel was added at the Ninth and C Street location, stained-glass windows were added to the archways from the patio that was enclosed. The above photograph shows the chapel that was dedicated in March 1950 and the stained-glass windows. The below photograph shows three of the stained-glass windows where they are currently on display at the Mission Valley church overlooking the plaza. All the stained-glass windows were moved from the Ninth and C Street site and preserved at the Mission Valley location.

BIBLIOGRAPHY AND SPONSORS

Anniversary Sunday—50 Years at Ninth and C Streets, 88 Years in San Diego. San Diego, CA. 1957.

A Church in Mission: History of First Methodist Church in San Diego. San Diego, CA. 1990.

Dedication of Sanctuary, Easter Sunday 1943, First Methodist Church 9th and C. San Diego, CA. 1943.

Erwine, Samuel D. *History of the First Methodist Church, 1869–1957.* San Diego, CA. 1957.

First Church Historical Society/Committee with contributions by Lucille Hildreth Wherry, Ethel D. Imel, and Dr. Richard H. Peerson. Church records and documents.

Knudtson, Violet Emslie. *Landmark of a Century—A Centennial History.* San Diego, CA: Arts & Crafts Press, 1969.

Seventy-fifth Anniversary, 1869–1944, First Methodist Church of San Diego. San Diego, CA. 1944.

Thank you to the sponsors who made a financial contribution toward this book:

GOLD SPONSORS: Philip and Elaine Amerson; Dorothy Appleby; Kathee Christensen; Greg and Lyn Cobb; Kevin and Brandy Crislip; Robert and Demetra Divine; Arleigh and Linda Dotson; John Hermann; Raymond Homan; Jim and Joanne Jackson; Karon Jarrard; Rev. Kevin Jones; Ed and Erica Knowles; Dan and Maria Lai; David Latham; Homer and Linda Moyer; Abby Sailors; Jessica, Tim, and Abigail Strysko; Dione and Nick Taylor; Jason Tucker; Dave Watters; Cindy Whitmore; and Joyce Wright.

SILVER SPONSORS: Steve and Carol Ames, Audrey Blevins, Louise Cavallin, Ramona Court, Marlene Giles and Michelle Trujillo, Dick and Marlys Hamann, Beckie Henselmeier, Elizabeth Holcomb, Philip and Sharon Jeter, The Kirk-Clark family, Martha McPhail, Brian and Pamela Murray, Thomas and Eleene Myers, Lois Nelson, Gloria Patten-Lane, Carole Porter, John and Jan Roese, Debra and Joseph Rosevear, Lembi Saarmann, Stefanie and Kyle Scroggins, Robin and Connie Smith, Patricia Twyman, and Rev. Molly Vetter and Matthew Parker.

DISCOVER THOUSANDS OF LOCAL HISTORY BOOKS FEATURING MILLIONS OF VINTAGE IMAGES

Arcadia Publishing, the leading local history publisher in the United States, is committed to making history accessible and meaningful through publishing books that celebrate and preserve the heritage of America's people and places.

Find more books like this at
www.arcadiapublishing.com

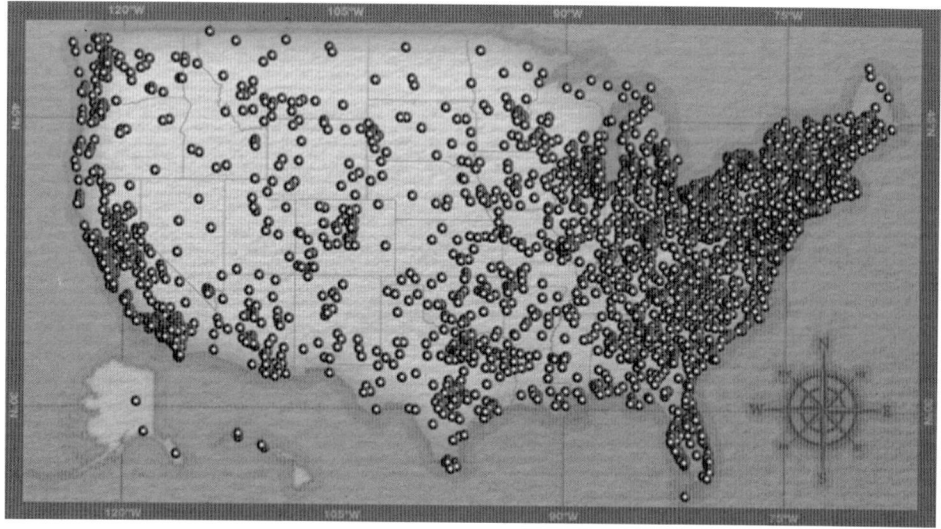

Search for your hometown history, your old stomping grounds, and even your favorite sports team.

Consistent with our mission to preserve history on a local level, this book was printed in South Carolina on American-made paper and manufactured entirely in the United States. Products carrying the accredited Forest Stewardship Council (FSC) label are printed on 100 percent FSC-certified paper.